SpringerBriefs in Computer Science

T0236531

Jie Yang • Yingying Chen • Wade Trappe
Jerry Cheng

Pervasive Wireless Environments: Detecting and Localizing User Spoofing

 Springer

Jie Yang
Department of Computer Science and Engineering
Oakland University
Rochester
Michigan
USA

Yingying Chen
Department Electrical & Computer Engineering
Stevens Institute of Technology
Hoboken
New Jersey
USA

Wade Trappe
Wireless Information Network Lab
Rutgers, The State University
 of New Jersey
North Brunswick
New Jersey, USA

Jerry Cheng
Rutgers, The State University
 of New Jersey
New Brunswick
New Jersey
USA

ISSN 2191-5768   ISSN 2191-5776 (electronic)
ISBN 978-3-319-07355-2   ISBN 978-3-319-07356-9 (eBook)
DOI 10.1007/978-3-319-07356-9
Springer Cham Heidelberg New York Dordrecht London

Library of Congress Control Number: 2014940861

Printed on acid-free paper

Springer is part of Springer Science + Business Media (www.springer.com)

Preface

As more wireless and sensor networks are deployed, information provided and shared by wireless systems has become an inseparable part of our social fabric. However, wireless security is often cited as a major technical barrier that must be overcome before widespread adoption of wireless information systems. Due to the shared nature of the wireless medium, adversaries can gather useful identity information during passive monitoring and further utilize the identity information to perform user spoofing. During an user spoofing attack, an adversary can forge its identity to masquerade as another device, or even creates multiple illegitimate identities in the networks. For instance, in Wi-Fi network, it is easy for an attacker to modify its MAC address of network interface card (NIC) to another device through vendor-supplied NIC drivers or open-source NIC drivers. In addition, by masquerading as an authorized wireless access point or as an authorized client, an attacker can launch denial of service attacks, bypass access control mechanisms, or falsely advertise services to wireless clients.

Attacks originated from user spoofing will have a serious impact on the successful deployment of pervasive wireless environments. It is thus desirable to detect the presence of user spoofing and eliminate it from the network. The traditional approach to prevent user spoofing is to apply cryptographic authentication. However, authentication requires additional key management infrastructural overhead and extra computational power associated with distributing, and maintaining cryptographic keys. Due to the limited power and resources available on the wireless devices and the dynamics introduced by the node mobility, it is not always possible to deploy authentication. This book provides a different approach by using the physical properties associated with wireless transmissions to detect the presence of user spoofing. The book begins by introducing user spoofing in wireless networks, presenting the motivation of the book and summarizing our contributions of the book. After that, we discuss the feasibility of launching user spoofing attacks and their impact on the pervasive wireless environments in Chap. 2. In Chap. 3, we describe the attack detection model that exploits the spatial correlation of Received Signal Strength (RSS) inherited from wireless devices as a foundation. This chapter further presents the performance evaluation of the spoofing attack detection model through experiments in practical environments. In Chap. 4, we deal with the situation when multiple spoofing attackers are present. We develop a statistical approach to determine the number of attackers, and further show how to localize these adversaries. Both the attacker number determination and adversaries localization methods are evaluated though two wireless testbeds including both Wi-Fi and Zigbee networks. In Chap. 5, we study user spoofing under mobile wireless networks. For many people, mobile devices are becoming the favored portal to their online social lives. Thus, the identity fraud conducted by malicious mobile agents will have detrimental impact on the successful deployment of mobile pervasive applications. We develop the DEMOTE system, which exploits the correlation within the RSS trace based on each devices identity to detect mobile attackers in Chap. 5. The DEMOTE system is evaluated in an office environment in both Wi-Fi and Zigbee networks. In Chap. 6, we provide an overview of the state-of-the-art research. Finally, the conclusions and future directions are presented in Chap. 7.

Contents

Chapter 1
Introduction

1.1 Background and Motivation

As computing and networking shift from the static model of the wired Internet toward the new and exciting anytime-anywhere service model of the mobile Internet, information will be gathered by wireless devices and made available to mobile users to consume or process on-the-go. However, wireless security is often cited as a major technical barrier that must be overcome before widespread adoption of such wireless information systems to support a broad array of pervasive applications including emergency rescue and recovery, asset monitoring and tracking, mobile social networks, smart healthcare, and battlefield protection.

Due to the openness of the wireless transmission medium, adversaries can monitor any transmission. Further, adversaries can easily purchase low-cost wireless devices and use these commonly-available platforms to launch a variety of attacks with little effort. Among various types of attacks, identity-based spoofing attacks are especially easy to launch and can cause significant damage to network performance. For instance, in an 802.11 network, it is easy for an attacker to gather useful MAC address information during passive monitoring and then modify its MAC address by simply issuing an *ifconfig* command to masquerade as another device. In spite of existing 802.11 security techniques including Wired Equivalent Privacy (WEP), Wi-Fi Protected Access (WPA), or 802.11i (WPA2), such methodology can only protect data frames-an attacker can still spoof management or control frames to cause significant impact on networks.

Spoofing attacks can further facilitate a variety of traffic injection attacks [1, 2], such as attacks on access control lists, rogue access point attacks, and eventually Denial-of-Service (DoS) attacks. A broad survey of possible spoofing attacks can be found in [3, 4]. Moreover, in a large-scale network, multiple adversaries may masquerade as the same identity and collaborate to launch malicious attacks such as network resource utilization attack and denial-of-service attack quickly. Therefore, it is important to (1) detect the presence of spoofing attacks, (2) determine the number of attackers, and (3) localize multiple adversaries and eliminate them.

Furthermore, for many people mobile devices are becoming the favored portal to their online social lives. People are using their phones to read news, publish

J. Yang et al., *Pervasive Wireless Environments: Detecting and Localizing User Spoofing,*
SpringerBriefs in Computer Science, DOI 10.1007/978-3-319-07356-9_1,
© The Author(s) 2014

photos, perform banking transactions, play games, and check on friends. More than 250 million users access Facebook on their mobile devices, and 40 % of all tweets come from mobile platforms. Thus, identity fraud performed by malicious mobile agents will inflict security and privacy damages on the social life of the individual who carries wireless devices. Detecting identity fraud launched by mobile agents is important as it allows the network to further exploit a wide range of defense strategies in different network layers, and consequently helps to ensure secure and trustworthy communication in emerging mobile pervasive computing.

Inspired by utilizing opportunities provided by the advancement of wireless technologies and the unique characteristics of spatial correlation enabled by the ubiquitous wireless infrastructures, we develop techniques and systems that aim to enhance wireless security by defending against identity spoofing attacks in wireless networks. Specifically, we exploit spatial correlation of Received Signal Strength (RSS) inherent from wireless device to enhance wireless security. This approach has the capability to work with any wireless networks and devices, and complement conventional security solutions. We first addressed identity-based spoofing attacks in static wireless environments. Because they are especially harmful as the claimed identity of a wireless device is often considered as an important first step in an adversary's attempt to launch a variety of attacks. We further deal with the situation when multiple spoofing attackers masquerading as the same device identity. We then focus on the problem of detecting identity fraud performed by mobile agents through exploiting the time series based RSS traces.

1.2 Contributions

The contributions of our work are listed below. We first proposed an attack detection model that exploits the spatial correlation of Received Signal Strength (RSS) inherited from wireless devices for detecting identity-based spoofing attacks. Specifically, we formulated the attack detection problem as a statistical significance testing problem. We further utilized the clustering analysis to derive the test statistic for attack detection. Determining the number of adversaries that masquerade as the same device identity is a particularly challenging problem, which enables us to further localize multiple adversaries. Two cluster-based mechanisms, namely Silhouette Plot and System Evolution, are developed to determine the number of attackers. Moreover, we developed the SILENCE mechanism that employs the minimum distance testing of RSS values in addition to cluster analysis and can achieve better accuracy than other methods under study that merely use cluster analysis alone. When the training data is available, we explored using the Support Vector Machines (SVM) method to further improve the accuracy of determining the number of attackers. In addition, we developed an integrated detection and localization system that can localize the positions of multiple attackers in order to eliminate the adversaries from the network. We conducted experiments on two testbeds through both an 802.11 network (Wi-Fi) and an 802.15.4 (ZigBee) network in two real office building environments.

We found that our detection mechanisms are highly effective in detecting the presence of spoofing attacks with detection rates over 98 % and determining the number of adversaries, achieving over 90 % hit rates and precision simultaneously when using SILENCE and SVM-based mechanism. Based on the number of attackers determined by our mechanisms, our integrated detection and localization system can localize adversaries even when attackers using different transmission power levels. The performance of localizing adversaries achieves similar results as those under normal conditions, thereby, providing strong evidence of the effectiveness of our approach in detecting wireless identity-based attacks, determining the number of attackers and localizing adversaries.

Further, we proposed an approach to detect identity fraud attacks in mobile wireless environments. We develop the DEMOTE system, which exploits the correlation within the RSS trace based on each node's identity to perform attack detection in either the signal space or the physical space. The proposed DEMOTE system utilizes an optimal thresholding scheme to partition the RSS readings of each node's identity, and further reconstruct the RSS traces over time for attack detection. We found that under normal (non-attack) situations the reconstructed RSS traces are highly correlated since the traces are originated from one mobile device, whereas under a spoofing attack the RSS traces are much less correlated because of the presence of the spoofing node that is not moving together with the victim node. Our approach does not require any changes or cooperation from wireless devices other than packet transmissions. Through experiments from an office building environment, we show that DEMOTE achieves accurate attack detection both in signal space as well as in physical space using localization and is generic across different technologies including IEEE 802.11 b/g and IEEE 802.15.4.

Our research work serves as a pioneer's effort to explore using the unique wireless property, spatial correlation, as a useful characteristic associated with each wireless device to address security problems. The proposed research work highlights the importance of new paradigms for securing future wireless systems that takes advantage of unique wireless-specific properties to thwart security threats without requiring overhead to wireless devices.

1.3 Outline of the Book

The rest of the book is organized as follows. In Chap. 2, we discuss the feasibility of launching user spoofing attacks and their impact on the pervasive wireless environments. In Chap. 3, we describe the attack detection model that exploits the spatial correlation of Received Signal Strength (RSS) inherited from wireless devices as a foundation. This chapter further presents the performance evaluation of the spoofing attack detection model through experiments in practical environments. In Chap. 4, we deal with the situation when multiple spoofing attackers masquerading as the same device identity. We develop a statistical approach to determine the number of attackers, and further show how to localize these adversaries. In Chap. 5, we study

Chapter 2
Feasibility of Launching User Spoofing

We provide a brief overview of identity-based spoofing attack, and its impact to the wireless and sensor networks in this chapter.

As more wireless and sensor networks are deployed, they will increasingly become tempting targets for malicious attacks. Due to the shared nature of the wireless medium, attackers can gather useful identity information during passive monitoring and further utilize the identity information to launch identity-based attacks, in particular, the most harmful but easy to launch attack: *spoofing attacks*.

In an user-spoofing attack, an attacker can forge its identity to masquerade as another device, or even creates illegitimate identities in the networks. For instance, in an 802.11 network, it is easy for an attacker to modify its MAC address of network interface card (NIC) to another device through vendor-supplied NIC drivers or open-source NIC drivers. In addition, by masquerading as an authorized wireless access point or as an authorized client, an attacker can launch denial of service attacks, bypass access control mechanisms, or falsely advertise services to wireless clients. The 802.11 protocol suite provides insufficient identity verification during message exchange, including most control and management frames. Therefore, the adversary can utilize this weakness and request various services as if it were another user. Identity-based spoofing attacks are a serious threat in the network since they represent a form of identity compromise and can facilitate a series of traffic injection attacks, including spoofing-based denial-of-service (DoS) attacks.

For instance, an adversary can launch a deauthetication attack. After a client chooses an access point for future communication, it must authenticate itself to the access point before the communication session starts. Both the client and the access point are allowed to explicitly request for deauthentication to void the existing authentication relationship with each other. Unfortunately, this deauthentication message is not authenticated. Therefore, an attacker can spoof this deauthentication message, either on behalf of the client, or on behalf of the access point [1, 2]. The adversary can persistently repeat this attack and completely prevent the client from transmitting or receiving.

Further, an attacker can utilize identity spoofing and launch the Rogue Access Point (AP) attack against the wireless network. In the Rogue AP attack, the adversary first sets up a rogue access point with the same MAC address and SSID as the legitimate access point, but with a stronger signal. When a station enters the coverage of the rogue AP, the default network configuration will make the station automatically associate with the rogue access point, which has a stronger signal. Then the adversary can take actions to influence the communication. For example, it can direct fake traffic to the associated station or drop the requests made by the station. Besides the basic packet flooding attacks, the adversary can make use of identity-spoofing to perform more sophisticated flooding attacks on access points, such as probe request, authentication request, and association request flooding attacks [3].

Therefore, the identity-based spoofing attacks will significantly impact the network performance. The conventional approaches to address identity-based attacks use authentication. However, the application of authentication requires reliable key distribution, management, and maintenance mechanisms. It is not always desirable to apply authentication because of its infrastructural, computational, and management overhead. Further, cryptographic methods are susceptible to node compromise—a serious concern as most wireless nodes are easily accessible, allowing their memory to be easily scanned.

Thus, it is desirable to use properties that do not require overheads and changes on nodes and cannot be undermined even when nodes are compromised. We propose to use Received Signal Strength (RSS), a property associated with the transmission and reception of communication (and hence not reliant on cryptography), as the basis for detecting identity-based attacks. Employing RSS as a means to detect spoofing attacks will not require any additional cost to the wireless devices themselves—they will merely use their existing communication methods, while the wireless network will use a collection of access points to monitor received signal strength for the potential of identity-based attacks. Our proposed techniques will handle the problem of unreliable and time-varying nature of RSS [4, 5]. These techniques will also address the issues when an attacker varies its transmission power to launch attacks and trick the system.

References

1. J. Bellardo and S. Savage, "802.11 denial-of-service attacks: Real vulnerabilities and practical solutions," in *Proceedings of the USENIX Security Symposium*, 2003, pp. 15–28.
2. W. A. Arbaugh, N. Shankar, Y. Wan, and K. Zhang "Your 802.11 network has no clothes," *IEEE Wireless Communications*, vol. 9, no. 6, pp. 44–51, Dec. 2002.
3. F. Ferreri, M. Bernaschi, and L. Valcamonici "Access points vulnerabilities to dos attacks in 802.11 networks," in *Proceedings of the IEEE Wireless Communications and Networking Conference*, 2004.
4. G. Zhou, T. He, S. Krishnamurthy, and J. A. Stankovic, "Models and solutions for radio irregularity in wireless sensor networks," *ACM Transactions on Sensor Networks*, vol. 2, pp. 221–262, 2006.
5. A. Krishnakumar and P. Krishnan, "On the accuracy of signal strength-based location estimation techniques," in *Proceedings of the IEEE International Conference on Computer Communications (INFOCOM)*, March 2005.

Chapter 3
Attack Detection Model

User spoofing has a serious impact to the normal operation of wireless and sensor networks. It is thus desirable to detect the presence of identity-based attacks and eliminate them from the network. The traditional approach to address identity-based attacks is to apply cryptographic authentication. However, authentication requires additional infrastructural overhead and computational power associated with distributing, and maintaining cryptographic keys. Due to the limited power and resources available to the wireless devices and sensor nodes, it is not always possible to deploy authentication. In this chapter, we take a different approach by using the physical properties associated with wireless transmissions to detect identity-based attacks. Specifically, we utilizes the Received Signal Strength (RSS) measured across a set of landmarks (i.e., reference points with known locations) to perform detection of identity-based attacks. In this chapter, We focus on static nodes, which are common for most identity-based attacks scenarios [1]. Our scheme does not add any overhead to the wireless devices and sensor nodes.

We formulate a generalized attack detection model using statistical significance testing. We then provide theoretical analysis of exploiting the spatial correlation of RSS inherited from wireless nodes for attack detection. In our theoretical analysis, we first derived the mathematical relationship between the distance of RSS in signal space and the node distance in physical space. We then developed the analytical expression of the detection rate, false positive rate of determining whether two nodes are resided at the same location based on the RSS distance in signal space. The theoretical analysis provides both the theoretical support on detecting identity-based attacks using the spatial correlation of RSS as well as the analytic results on detection effectiveness.

Further, by examining the clustering effects of RSS over time in signal space, we found that the distance between the centroids of clusters derived by the clustering algorithm in signal space is a good test statistic for effective attack detection.

To evaluate the effectiveness of our attack detector, we conducted experiments using both an 802.11 network as well as an 802.15.4 network in two real office building environments. We evaluated the performance of our attack detector using detection rate and receiver operating characteristic curve. We found that the performance of the attack detector is inline with the analytical results, suggesting that our attack detector is highly effective with over 95 % detection rates and under 5 % false positive rates.

J. Yang et al., *Pervasive Wireless Environments: Detecting and Localizing User Spoofing,*
SpringerBriefs in Computer Science, DOI 10.1007/978-3-319-07356-9_3,
© The Author(s) 2014

The rest of the chapter is organized as follows. In Sect. 3.1, we formulate the detection problem of identity-based attacks. In Sect. 3.2, we provide theoretical analysis of using the spatial correlation of RSS for attack detection. In Sect. 3.3, we propose our cluster-analysis based attack detector for spoofing attacks detection. We next describe our experimental methodology in Sect. 3.4. We present the performance evaluation of detecting spoofing attacks in Sect. 3.5. Finally, we present summary in Sect. 3.6.

3.1 Formulation of Attack Detection

RSS is widely available in deployed wireless communication networks and its values are closely correlated with location in physical space. In addition, RSS is a common physical property used by a widely diverse set of localization algorithms [2–5]. In spite of its several meter-level localization accuracy, using RSS is an attractive approach because it can reuse the existing wireless infrastructure, and it is sufficient to meet the accuracy requirement of most applications. For example, during the health care monitoring, the doctor may only need to know which room the tracked patient is residing. We thus derive an attack detector for identity-based attacks utilizing properties of the RSS.

We formulate attack detection as a statistical significance testing problem, where the null hypothesis is

$$\mathcal{H}_0 : \text{normal (no attack).}$$

In significance testing, a test statistic $\mathbf{T}$ is used to evaluate whether observed data belongs to the null-hypothesis or not. For a particular significance level, α (defined as the probability of rejecting the hypothesis if it is true), there is a corresponding *acceptance region* Ω such that we declare the null hypothesis valid if an observed value of the test statistic $\mathbf{T}^{\mathbf{obs}} \in \Omega$, and reject the null hypothesis if $\mathbf{T}^{\mathbf{obs}} \notin \Omega$ (i.e. declare an attack is present if $\mathbf{T}^{\mathbf{obs}} \in \Omega^c$, where Ω^c is the *critical region* of the test). In our attack detection problem, the region Ω and decision rule is specified according to the form of the detection statistic $\mathbf{T}$ (for example, when using distance in signal strength space for $\mathbf{T}$, the decision rule becomes comparison against a threshold), and rejection of the null hypothesis corresponds to declaring the presence of an attack.

3.2 Theoretical Analysis of the Spatial Correlation of RSS

The challenge in identity-based attacks detection is to devise strategies that use the uniqueness of spatial information, but not using location directly as the attackers' positions are unknown. We propose to study RSS, a property closely correlated with location in physical space and is readily available in the existing wireless networks.

Although affected by random noise, environmental bias, and multipath effects, the RSS measured at a set of landmarks (i.e., reference points with known locations) is closely related to the transmitter's physical location and is governed by the distance to the landmarks [6]. The RSS readings at the same physical location are stable over time, whereas the RSS readings at different locations in physical space are distinctive. Thus, the RSS readings present strong spatial correlation characteristics.

We define the RSS value vector as $s = \{s_1, s_2, \ldots s_n\}$ where n is the number of landmarks/access points (APs) that are monitoring the RSS of the wireless nodes and know their locations. Generally, the RSS at a landmark from a wireless node is lognormally distributed [7]:

$$s_i(d_j)[dBm] = P(d_0)[dBm] - 10\gamma \log\left(\frac{d_j}{d_0}\right) + X_i, \qquad (3.1)$$

where i is the ith landmark, $P(d_0)$ represents the transmitting power of the node at the reference distance d_0, d_j is the distance between the wireless node j and the ith landmark, and γ is the path loss exponent, X_i is the shadow fading which follows zero mean Gaussian distribution with δ standard deviation [7, 8]. For simplicity, we assume the wireless nodes have the same transmission power. We will discuss the issue of using different transmission power levels in Sect. 3.5. Given two wireless nodes in the physical space, the RSS distance between two nodes in signal space at the ith landmark is given by

$$\Delta s_i = 10\gamma \log\left(\frac{d_2}{d_1}\right) + \Delta X, \qquad (3.2)$$

where ΔX follows zero mean Gaussian distribution with $\sqrt{2}\delta$ standard deviation. According to Eq. (3.2), when the two wireless nodes are at the same location (i.e., $d_1 = d_2$), the RSS distance in signal space at the ith landmark follows a normal distribution with zero mean and $\sqrt{2}\delta$ standard deviation. Whereas the distance follows a normal distribution with $10\gamma \log(d_2/d_1)$ mean and $\sqrt{2}\delta$ standard deviation if these two nodes are at different locations.

The square of RSS distance in n-dimensional signal space (i.e. at n landmarks) is then determined by

$$\Delta D^2 = \sum_{i=1}^{n} \Delta s_i^2, \qquad (3.3)$$

where Δs_i with $i = 1, 2 \ldots, n$ is the RSS distance at ith landmark and is given by Eq. (3.2).

Based on the Eqs. (3.2) and (3.3), we know that, when these two wireless nodes are at the same location, the distance $(1/2\delta^2)\Delta D^2$ in n dimension signal space follows a *central Chi-square distribution* $\chi^2(n)$ with n degree of freedom [9]. The probability density functions (PDF) of the random variable $X = \Delta D^2$, which is the square distance in n-dimensional signal space, when two wireless nodes are at the same location can be represented as:

$$f_X(x|\text{same location}) = \frac{1}{2^n \delta^n \Gamma(n/2)} e^{-x/4\delta^2} x^{(n/2-1)}, \qquad (3.4)$$

where $x \geq 0$ and $\Gamma(n/2)$ denotes the Gamma function, which has closed-form values at the half-integers.

However, when these two wireless nodes are at different locations, $(1/2\delta^2)\Delta D^2$ becomes a *non-central chi-square distribution* $\chi^2(n,\lambda)$ with n degree of freedom and a non-centrality parameter λ, where

$$\lambda = \sum_{i=1}^{n} \left(10\gamma \, \log\left(\frac{d_{i2}}{d_{i1}}\right) \right)^2, \tag{3.5}$$

and d_{ij}, with $i = 1, 2, \ldots n., j = 1, 2.$, is the distance from jth wireless nodes to the ith landmark. The PDF of the random variable $X = \Delta D^2$ when two wireless node are at the different locations can be represented as:

$$f_X(x|\text{diff. locations}) = \frac{1}{4\delta^2} e^{-\frac{\lambda+x}{4\delta^2}} \left(\frac{x}{\lambda}\right)^{\frac{n-2}{4}} I_{\frac{n-2}{2}}\left(\frac{\sqrt{\lambda x}}{2\delta^2}\right), \tag{3.6}$$

where $I_\alpha(z)$ is a modified Bessel function of the first kind [9].

Given the threshold τ, the probability that we can determine the two nodes are at different locations in a two dimensional physical space with n landmarks (i.e. detection rate DR) is given by

$$DR = P(x > \tau|\text{diff. locations}) = 1 - \mathcal{F}_{\chi^2(n,\lambda/2\delta^2)}\left(\frac{\tau}{2\delta^2}\right), \tag{3.7}$$

and the corresponding false positive rate is

$$FPR = P(x > \tau|\text{same locations}) = 1 - \mathcal{F}_{\chi^2(n)}\left(\frac{\tau}{2\delta^2}\right), \tag{3.8}$$

where $\mathcal{F}_X(\cdot)$ is the CDF of the random variable X.

From Eqs. (3.7) and (3.8), for a specified detection rate DR, the threshold of test can be obtained as

$$\tau = 2\delta^2 \mathcal{F}_{\chi^2(n,\lambda/2\delta^2)}^{-1}(1 - DR), \tag{3.9}$$

and the false positive rate can be represented in terms of the detection rate

$$FPR = 1 - \mathcal{F}_{\chi^2(n)}\left(\mathcal{F}_{\chi^2(n,\lambda/2\delta^2)}^{-1}(1 - DR)\right). \tag{3.10}$$

From Eq. (3.7), we can see that the detection rate DR increases with λ, which can be represented by the distance between two wireless nodes together with the landmarks. Moreover, for a specified detection rate DR, Eq. (3.10) shows that the false positive rate FPR increases with the standard deviation of shadowing δ.

We next study the detection power of our approach by using the RSS-based spatial correlation. Figure 3.1 presents the numerical results of receiver operating characteristic (ROC) curves based on Eqs. (3.7) and (3.8) when randomly placing two wireless devices in a 100×100 feet square area. There are four landmarks deployed at the four corners of the square area. The physical distance between two wireless devices is 16 feet, 20 feet and 25 feet, respectively. The path loss exponent γ is set to 2.5

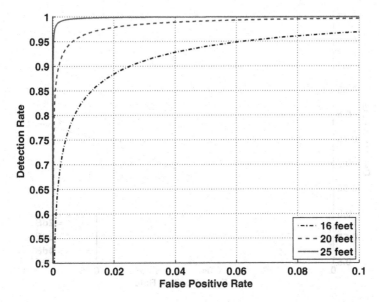

Fig. 3.1 The ROC curves when the distance between two wireless devices is 16 feet, 20 feet and 25 feet, respectively. The standard deviation of shadowing is 2dB. The path loss exponent is 2.5

and the standard deviation of shadowing is 2dB. From the figure, we observed that the ROC curves shift to the upper left when increasing the distance between two devices. This indicates that the farther away the two nodes are separated, the better detection performance that our method can achieve. This is because the detection performance is proportional to the non-centrality parameter λ, which is represented by the distance between two wireless nodes together with the landmarks.

We further investigate the detection performance of our approach under RSS variations. In this study, we fixed the distance between two wireless devices as 25 feet. The obtained ROC curves when the standard deviation of shadowing is set to $2dB$, $3dB$ and $4dB$, respectively is shown in Fig. 3.2. From the figure, it can be seen that we can obtain better detection performance with lower standard deviation of shadowing δ. A larger standard deviation of shadowing causes the two distributions, i.e. non-central chi-square and central chi-square to get closer to one another. Consequently, the smaller standard deviation of shadowing δ results in a better detection performance.

3.3 Detection Philosophy

The above analysis provides the theoretical support of using the spatial correlation in RSS inherited from wireless nodes to perform attack detection. It also showed that the RSS readings from a wireless node over time fluctuate under different σ and should cluster together. In particular, the RSS readings from the same physical location

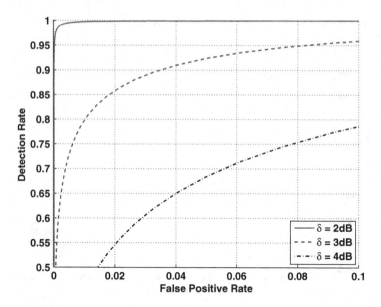

Fig. 3.2 The ROC curves when the standard deviation of shadowing is $2dB, 3dB$ and $4dB$, respectively. The distance between two devices is 25 feet

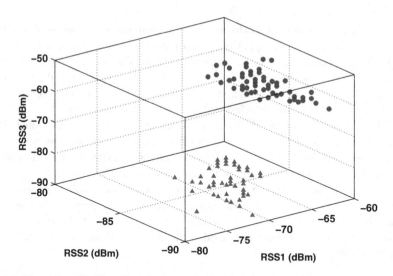

Fig. 3.3 Illustration of RSS readings from two physical locations

over time will belong to the same cluster points in the n-dimensional signal space, while the RSS readings from different locations over time should form different clusters in signal space as shown in Fig. 3.3, which presents RSS reading vectors of three landmarks (i.e., $n = 3$) from two different physical locations. This observation suggests that we may conduct cluster analysis on top of RSS readings to find out the distance in signal space in practice. Further, we can detect the identity-based attacks based on the observed RSS distance between clusters.

In this work, we utilize the Partitioning Around Medoids (PAM) Method to perform clustering analysis in RSS. The PAM Method [10] is a popular iterative descent clustering algorithm. The PAM method arbitrarily chooses K sample points as the initial medoids if we partition the data set into K clusters. It then subsequently swaps new sample points as new medoids to reduce the cost of the objective function, which is the sum of the dissimilarities of all the sample points to their nearest medoid:

$$J_{min} = \sum_{j=1}^{K} \sum_{\mathbf{s_n} \in C_j} \|\mathbf{s_n} - \mathbf{M_j}\|^2, \qquad (3.11)$$

where $\mathbf{s_n}$ is a RSS vector representing the nth sample point and M_j is the sample point that is chosen as the medoid for the jth cluster C_j in signal space. Compared to the popular K-means method [11], the PAM method is more robust in the presence of noise and outliers. Thus, the PAM method is more suitable in determining clusters from RSS streams, which can be unreliable and fluctuating over time due to random noise and environmental bias [12].

Under normal conditions, when examining the RSS stream from a node identity, the distance between the centroids from PAM cluster analysis in signal space should be close to each other since there is basically only one cluster from a single physical location. However, under a spoofing attack, there is more than one node at different physical locations claiming the same node identity. As a result, when examining the RSS stream over time from a node identity, the RSS sample readings from the attacked node (i.e., the original node) will be mixed with RSS readings from at least one different location. Thus, more than one clusters will be formed in the signal space and the distance between the centroids is larger (i.e., $\mathbf{T^{obs}} > \tau$) as the centroids are derived from the different RSS clusters associated with different locations (the original node plus spoofing nodes) in physical space. When the RSS reading vectors as shown in Fig. 3.3 is from one wireless node identity, we observed that two RSS clusters are formed and the distance between two centroids is large. This clearly indicates that the RSS readings are coming from two different physical locations and thus declares the presence of a spoofing attack. Further, based on our analysis in Sect. 3.2, the farther the attacker is from the original node, the more likely their RSS patterns differ significantly and the higher accuracy the detector may achieve.

3.4 Experimental Methodology

3.4.1 Experimental Setup

In order to evaluate the effectiveness of our mechanisms to detect identity-based attacks, we conducted experiments using two networks: an 802.11 (Wi-Fi) network at the Wireless Information Network Laboratory (WINLAB) and an 802.15.4 (ZigBee) network in the Computer Science Department at Rutgers University. The size of these two floors are 219×169 ft and 200×80 ft respectively. Figure 3.4a shows the 802.11 (Wi-Fi) network with five landmarks shown in red stars deployed to maximize signal strength coverage in the yellow-shaded experimental area. Whereas the 802.15.4 (ZigBee) network is presented in Fig. 3.4b with four landmarks distributed in a squared setup in order to achieve optimal landmark placement [6] as shown in red triangles.

The small dots in floor maps are the locations used for testing. For the 802.11 network, there are 101 locations and we collected 300 packet-level RSS samples at each location, while for the 802.15.4 network, there are 94 locations and 300 packet-level RSS samples are collected at each location.

To test our approach's ability to detect identity-based attacks, we randomly chose a point pair on the floor and treated one point as the position of the original node, and the other as the position of the spoofing node. We ran the identity-based attack detection test through all the possible combinations of point pairs on the floor using all the testing locations in both networks. There are total 5050 pairs for the 802.11 network and 4371 pairs for the 802.15.4 network.

3.4.2   Metrics

In this section, we present our metrics that will be used to evaluate the performance of our attack detector using spatial correlation of RSS based on the cluster analysis in real experiments.

Detection Rate and False Positive Rate An identity-based attack will cause the significance test to reject $\mathcal{H}_0$. We are thus interested in the statistical characterization of the attack detection attempts over all the possible attacks on the floor. The detection rate is defined as the percentage of attack attempts that are determined to be under attack. Note that, when the attack is present, the detection rate corresponds to the probability of detection P_d, while under normal (non-attack) conditions it corresponds to the probability of declaring a false positive P_{fa}. The detection rate and false positive rate vary under different thresholds.

Receiver Operating Characteristic (ROC) Curve To evaluate an attack detection scheme we want to study the false positive rate P_{fa} and probability of detection P_d together. The ROC curve is a plot of attack detection accuracy against the false positive rate. It can be obtained by varying the detection thresholds. The ROC curve provides a direct means to measure the trade off between false-positives and correct detections.

Distance between Wireless Nodes In a spoofing attack, when a spoofing node is close to an original node, the resulting test statistic D_c^{obs} will not be large and may affect the decision of attack detection. Hence, we are interested in studying how the distance between two nodes affects the performance of our attack detector.

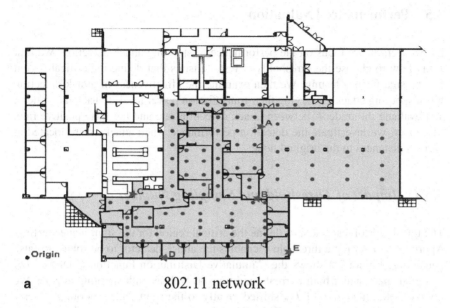

a 802.11 network

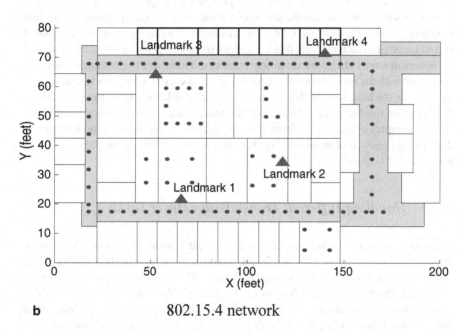

b 802.15.4 network

Fig. 3.4 Landmark setups and testing locations in two networks within two office buildings

3.5   Performance Evaluation

In this section, we focus on the performance of spoofing attack detection. We first study how to choose the thresholds of test statistics that define the critical region for the significance testing. We then examine the effectiveness of attack detection when spoofing attackers varying their transmission power levels to trick the system, and evaluate the tradeoff between attack detection rate and the false positive rate. Moreover, we investigate the detection performance when attackers are located at various distances to the original node.

3.5.1   Impact of Threshold and Sampling Number

The thresholds of test statistics define the critical region for the significance testing. Appropriately setting a threshold τ enables the attack detector to be robust to false detections. Figure 3.5 shows the Cumulative Distribution Function (CDF) of D_m in signal space under both normal conditions as well as with spoofing attacks. We observed that the curve of D_m shifted greatly to the right under spoofing attacks. Thus, when $D_m > \tau$, we can declare the presence of a spoofing attack. The short lines across the CDF lines are the averaged variances of D_m under different sampling numbers. We observed that the CDF curves of different sampling numbers are almost mixed together, which indicate that for a given threshold τ similar detection rate will be achieved under different sampling numbers. However, the averaged variance decreases with the increasing number of samples - the short-term RSS samples is not as stable as the long-term RSS samples. The more stable the D_m is, the more robust the detection mechanism can be. Therefore, there is a trade off between the number of RSS samples needed to perform spoofing detection and the time the system can declare the presence of an attack. For this study we use 200 RSS samples, which has a variance of $0.84 dB^2$.

3.5.2   Handling Different Transmission Power Levels

If a spoofing attacker sends packets at a different transmission power level from the original node, based on our cluster analysis there will be two distinct RSS clusters in signal space (i.e., D_m will be large). We varied transmission power for an attacker from $30 \, mW \, (15 dBm)$ to $1 \, mW \, (0 dBm)$. We found that in all cases D_m is larger than normal conditions. Figure 3.5b presents an example of the Cumulative Distribution Function (CDF) of the D_m for the 802.11 network when the spoofing attacker used transmission power of 10dB to send packets, whereas the original node used 15dB transmission power level. We observed that the curve of D_m under the different transmission power level shifts to the right indicating larger D_m values. Thus, spoofing attacks launched by using different transmission power levels will be detected effectively.

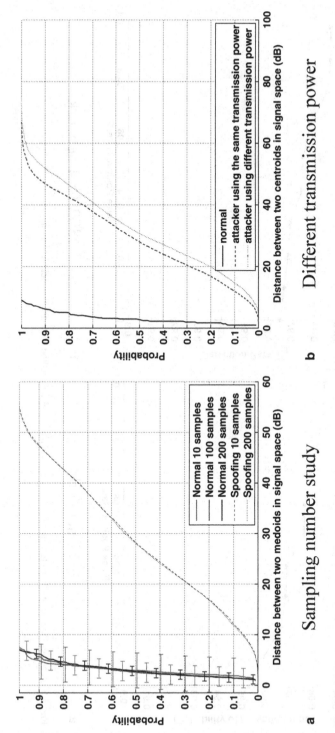

Fig. 3.5 802.11 network: Cumulative Distribution Function (CDF) of distance between medoids D_m in signal space

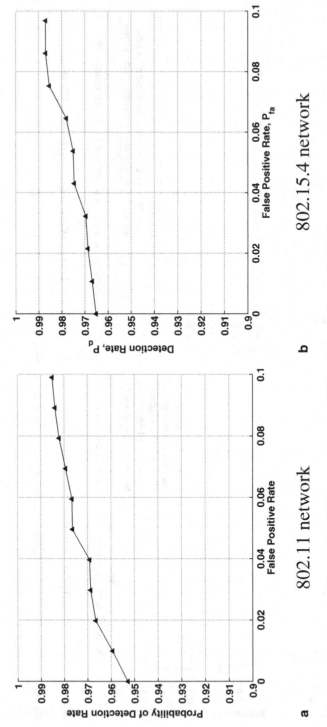

Fig. 3.6 Receiver Operating Characteristic (ROC) curves when using PAM method to perform attack detection

Table 3.1 Spoofing attack detection: Detection rate and false positive rate in two networks

Network	Threshold τ	Detection rate	False positive rate
802.11	6.2dB	0.985	0.10
802.11	7.3dB	0.976	0.05
802.11	9.1dB	0.953	0
802.15.4	7.6dB	0.987	0.10
802.15.4	9.0dB	0.975	0.05
802.15.4	12.4dB	0.965	0

3.5.3 Performance of Detection

Figure 3.6 presents the ROC curves of using D_m as a test statistic to perform attack detection for both the 802.11 and the 802.15.4 networks. Table 3.1 presents the detection rate and false positive rate for both networks under different threshold settings. The results are encouraging, showing that for false positive rates less than 10 %, the detection rate are above 98 % when the threshold τ is around $8dB$. Even when the false positive rate goes to zero, the detection rate is still more than 95 % for both networks.

3.5.4 Impact of Distance Between the Spoofing Node and the Original Node

We further study how likely a spoofing device can be detected by our attack detector when it is at various distances from the original node in physical space. Figure 3.7 presents the detection rate as a function of the distance between the spoofing node P_{spoof} and the original node P_{org}. We found that the further away P_{spoof} is from P_{org}, the higher the detection rate becomes. This observation is consistent with our theoretical analysis presented in Sect. 3.2. In particular, for the 802.11 network, the detection rate goes to over 90 % when P_{spoof} is about 15 feet away from P_{org} when the false positive rate is 5 %. While for the 802.15.4 network, the detection rate is above 90 % when the distance between P_{spoof} and P_{org} is about 20 feet by setting the false positive to 5 %. This is in line with the average localization estimation errors using RSS [4] which are about 15 feet. When the nodes are less than 15 feet apart, they have a high likelihood of generating similar RSS readings, and thus the spoofing detection rate falls below 90 %, but still greater than 70 %. However, when P_{spoof} moves closer to P_{org}, the attacker also increases the probability to expose itself. The detection rate goes to 100 % when the spoofing node is about 45–50 feet away from the original node.

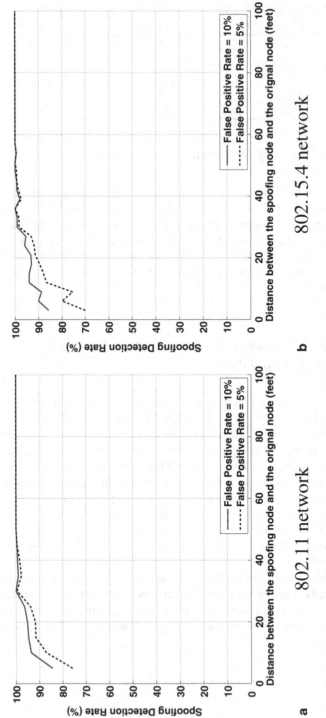

Fig. 3.7 The detection rate as a function of the distance between the spoofing node and the original node

3.6 Summary

In this chapter, we proposed a method for detecting identity-based spoofing attacks in wireless and sensor networks. In contrast to traditional identity-oriented authentication methods, our Receive Signal Strength (RSS) based approach does not add additional overhead to the wireless devices and sensor nodes. We formulated the identity-based detection problem as a statistical significance testing problem. We then provided theoretical analysis of exploiting the spatial correlation of RSS inherited from wireless nodes for attack detection. We further utilized the PAM cluster analysis to derive the test statistic. Our attack detector is robust to detect attacks launched by adversaries using different transmission power levels.

We studied the effectiveness and generality of our attack detector in both an 802.11 (Wi-Fi) network and an 802.15.4 (ZigBee) network in two real office building environments. The performance of the proposed attack detector is evaluated in terms of detection rates and receiver operating characteristic curves. Our attack detector has achieved high detection rates, over 95 % and low false positive rates, below 5 %.

References

1. Y. Sheng, K. Tan, G. Chen, D. Kotz, and A. Campbell, "Detecting 802.11 MAC layer spoofing using received signal strength," in *Proceedings of the IEEE International Conference on Computer Communications (INFOCOM)*, April 2008.
2. P. Bahl and V. N. Padmanabhan, "RADAR: An in-building RF-based user location and tracking system," in *Proceedings of the IEEE International Conference on Computer Communications (INFOCOM)*, March 2000, pp. 775–784.
3. M. Youssef, A. Agrawal, and A. U. Shankar, "WLAN location determination via clustering and probability distributions," in *Proceedings of the First IEEE International Conference on Pervasive Computing and Communications (PerCom)*, Mar. 2003, pp. 143–150.
4. Y. Chen, K. Kleisouris, X. Li, W. Trappe, and R. P. Martin, "The robustness of localization algorithms to signal strength attacks: a comparative study," in *Proceedings of the International Conference on Distributed Computing in Sensor Systems (DCOSS)*, June 2006, pp. 546–563.
5. T. Roos, P. Myllymaki, H. Tirri, P. Misikangas, and J. Sievanen, "A probabilistic approach to WLAN user location estimation," *International Journal of Wireless Information Networks*, vol. 9, no. 3, pp. 155–164, July 2002.
6. Y. Chen, J.-A. Francisco, W. Trappe, and R. P. Martin, "A practical approach to landmark deployment for indoor localization," in *Proceedings of the Third Annual IEEE Communications Society Conference on Sensor, Mesh and Ad Hoc Communications and Networks (IEEE SECON)*, September 2006.
7. A. Goldsmith, *Wireless Communications: Principles and Practice*. New York, NY, USA: Cambridge University Press, 2005.
8. T. Sarkar, Z. Ji, K. Kim, A. Medouri, and M. Salazar-Palma, "A survey of various propagation models for mobile communication," *Antennas and Propagation Magazine, IEEE*, vol. 45, no. 3, pp. 51–82, June 2003.
9. M. Abramowitz and I. A. Stegun, *Handbook of Mathematical Functions with Formulas, Graphs, and Mathematical Tables*. New York: Courier Dover, 1965.
10. L. Kaufman and P. J. Rousseeuw, *Finding Groups in Data: An Introduction to Cluster Analysis*. Wiley Series in Probability and Statistics, 1990.

11. Y. Chen, W. Trappe, and R. P. Martin, "Detecting and localizing wirelss spoofing attacks," in *Proceedings of the Fourth Annual IEEE Communications Society Conference on Sensor, Mesh and Ad Hoc Communications and Networks (SECON)*, May 2007.

12. G. Zhou, T. He, S. Krishnamurthy, and J. A. Stankovic, "Models and solutions for radio irregularity in wireless sensor networks," *ACM Transactions on Sensor Networks*, vol. 2, pp. 221–262, 2006.

Chapter 4
Detection and Localizing Multiple Spoofing Attackers

Under a malicious spoofing attack, multiple adversaries may masquerade as the same identity and collaborate to launch a denial-of-service attack quickly. Therefore, it is important to further determine the number of attackers that masquerade as the same identity in the wireless network. Further, detecting the presence of identity-based attacks in the network provides first order information towards defending against attackers. Learning the physical location of the attackers allows the network administrators to further exploit a wide range of defense strategies. For example, we can physically visit multiple adversaries and eliminate it from the network. We then explore how to find the positions of the adversaries by integrating our attack detector into a real-time indoor localization system.

We formulate the problem of determining the number of attackers as a multi-class detection problem. We then applied cluster based methods to determine the number of attacker. We further developed a mechanism called SILENCE for testing *Sil*houette Plot and System *E*volution with minimum distan*c*e of clusters, to improve the accuracy of determining the number of attackers. Additionally, when the training data is available, we propose to use Support Vector Machines (SVM) method to further improve the accuracy of determining the number of attackers.

Moreover, we developed an integrated localization system which utilizes the results of the number of attackers returned to further localize multiple adversaries. As we demonstrated through our experiments using both an 802.11 network as well as an 802.15.4 network in two real office building environments, the number of attack detection methods are highly effective in number of attackers detection with over 90 % hit rate and precision. Furthermore, using a set of representative localization algorithms, we show that our integrated localization system can achieve similar localization accuracy when localizing adversaries to that of under normal conditions. One key observation is that the integrated localization system can handle attackers using different transmission power levels, thereby providing strong evidence of the effectiveness of localizing adversaries when there are multiple attackers in the network.

The rest of the paper is organized as follows. We provide multiple spoofing attacker detection problem formulation in Sect. 4.1. We propose our cluster-analysis based mechanisms for number of attacker detection in Sect. 4.2. In Sect. 4.3, we present the integrated detection and localization system. Finally, we provide summary of this chapter in Sect. 4.4.

J. Yang et al., *Pervasive Wireless Environments: Detecting and Localizing User Spoofing*, SpringerBriefs in Computer Science, DOI 10.1007/978-3-319-07356-9_4, © The Author(s) 2014

4.1 Problem Formulation

After detecting the presence of a attack, the next phase is to determine the number of attackers, using the same node identity to launch spoofing attacks, so that we can further localize the multiple adversaries and eliminate them. We formulate the problem of determining the number of attackers as a multi-class detection problem, in which we want to identify how many clusters exist in the signal space for the RSS readings that associated with the same device idnetity. We describe below on how to quatify the number of attackers detection.

Inaccurate estimation of the number of attackers will cause failure in localizing the multiple adversaries. As we do not know how many adversaries will use the same node identity to launch attacks, determining the number of attackers becomes a multi-class detection problem and is similar to determining how many clusters exist in signal space for the same idenitity. If C is the set of all classes, i.e., all possible combination of number of attackers. For instance, $C = \{1, 2, 3, 4\}$. For a class of specific number of attackers c_i, e.g., $c_i = 3$, we define P_i as the positive class of c_i and all other classes (i.e., all other number of attackers) as negative class N_i:

$$P_i = c_i, \tag{4.1}$$

$$N_i = \bigcup_{j \neq i} c_j \in C. \tag{4.2}$$

Further, we are interested in the statistical characterization of the percentage that the number of attackers can be accurately determined over all possible testing attempts with mixed number of attackers. Associated with a specific number of attackers, i, we define the Hit Rate HR_i as $HR_i = \frac{N_{true}}{P_i}$ where N_{true} is the true positive detection of class c_i. Let N_{false} be the false detection of the class c_i out of the negative class N_i that do not have i number of attackers. We then define the false positive rate FP_i for a specific number of attackers of class c_i as $FP_i = \frac{N_{false}}{N_i}$. Then the Precision is defined as:

$$Precision_i = \frac{N_{true}}{N_{true} + N_{false}}. \tag{4.3}$$

F-measure F-measure is originated from information retrieval and measures the accuracy of a test by considering both the Hit Rate and the Precision [1]:

$$F - measure_i = \frac{2}{\frac{1}{Precision_i} + \frac{1}{Hit\ Rate_i}}. \tag{4.4}$$

Multi-class ROC graph We further use the multi-class ROC graph to measure the effectiveness of our mechanisms. Particularly, we use two methods [2]: class-reference based and benefit-error based. The class-reference based formulation produces C different ROC curves when handling C classes based on P_i and N_i. Further, in the C-class detection problem the traditional 2x2 confusion matrix, including

Fig. 4.1 Illustration of the construction of Silhouettes, $K = 3, j = 1$

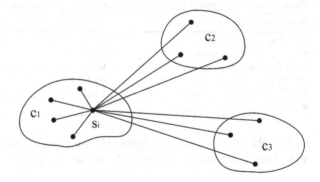

True Positives, False Positives, False Negatives, and True Negatives, becomes an CxC matrix, which contains the C benefits (true positives) and $C^2 - C$ possible errors (false positives). The benefit-error based method is based on the CxC matrix. For example, when $C = 3$ with possible number of attackers of $\{2, 3, 4\}$, the benefits are 3 and the possible errors are 6.

4.2 Attacker Number Determination

In this section, we first present two mechanisms, *Silhouette Plot* and *System Evolution* for number of attacker detection. Next, we describe the SILENCE mechanism that we developed, which performs an evaluation based on minimum cluster distance on top of the cluster analysis to improve the accuracy of determining the number of attackers. When the training data is available, we explore using SVM method to further improve the accuracy of determining the number of attackers.

4.2.1 Silhouette Plot

4.2.1.1 Attacker Number Determination

A Silhouette Plot is a graphical representation of a cluster [3]. To determine the number of attackers, we construct Silhouettes in the following way: the RSS sample points $\mathbf{S} = \{\mathbf{s}_1, \ldots, \mathbf{s}_N\}$ (with N as the total number of samples) are the data set and we let $C = (c_1, \ldots, c_K)$ be its clustering into K clusters. Let $d(\mathbf{s}_k, \mathbf{s}_l)$ be the distance between $\mathbf{s}_k$ and $\mathbf{s}_l$. Let $c_j = \left\{\mathbf{s}_1^j, \ldots, \mathbf{s}_{m_j}^j\right\}$ be the j-th cluster, $j = 1, \ldots, K$, where $m_j = |c_j|$. The average distance a_i^j between the i-th RSS vector in the cluster c_j and the other RSS vectors in the same cluster is thus given by:

$$a_i^j = \frac{1}{m_j - 1} \sum_{\substack{k=1 \\ k \neq i}}^{m_j} d\left(\mathbf{s}_i^j, \mathbf{s}_k^j\right), \quad i = 1, \ldots, m_j. \tag{4.5}$$

Table 4.1 Silhouette plot: hit rate, precision, and F-measure of determining the number of attackers

Number of attackers	2 (%)	3 (%)	4 (%)
802.11 network, hit rate	99.59	89.81	80.52
802.11 network, precision	91.85	87.29	99.33
802.11 network, F-measure	95.56	88.53	88.94
802.15.4 network, hit rate	99.46	91.05	83.77
802.15.4 network, precision	93.22	85.71	99.67
802.15.4 network, F-measure	96.24	88.30	91.03

Further, the minimum average distance between the i-th RSS vector in the cluster c_j and all the RSS vectors clustered in the clusters $c_k, k = 1, \ldots, K, k \neq j$ is given by:

$$b_i^j = \min_{\substack{n=1,\ldots K \\ n \neq j}} \left\{ \frac{1}{m_n} \sum_{k=1}^{m_n} d\left(s_i^j, s_k^n\right) \right\}, \quad i = 1, \ldots, m_j. \tag{4.6}$$

Then the silhouette width of the i-th RSS vector in the cluster c_j is defined as:

$$w_i^j = \frac{b_i^j - a_i^j}{\max\left\{a_i^j, b_i^j\right\}}. \tag{4.7}$$

From the Eq. (4.7), it follows that $-1 \leq w_i^j \leq 1$. We can now define the silhouette of the cluster c_j:

$$W_j = \frac{1}{m_j} \sum_{i=1}^{m_j} w_i^j. \tag{4.8}$$

Hence, the global Silhouette index for partition p that partitions the data set into K clusters is given by:

$$W(K)_p = \frac{1}{K} \sum_{j=1}^{K} w_j. \tag{4.9}$$

Finally, we define Silhouette Coefficient SC to determine the number of attackers:

$$SC = \max_K W(K)_p. \tag{4.10}$$

SC is used for the selection of a "best" value of the cluster number K (i.e., the optimal number of attackers) by choosing the K to make $W(K)$ as high as possible across all partitions. Since the objective of constructing silhouettes is to obtain SC, we note that there are no adjustable parameters in this detection scheme.

4.2.1.2 Experimental Evaluation

Table 4.1 presents experimental values of Hit Rate, Precision, and F-measure when the attacker number $i = \{2, 3, 4\}$ for both the 802.11 and the 802.15.4 networks. We observed that the performance of Silhouette Plot in both networks are qualitatively the same. We found that when the number of attackers equals to 2, i.e., 2 attackers masquerading the same identity in the network, the Silhouette Plot achieves both the highest Hit Rate, above 99 %, and the highest F-measure value, over 95 %. Further, the case of 4 attackers achieves the highest Precision above 99 %, which indicates that the detection of the number of attackers is more accurate, however, the Hit Rate decreases to about 80 %. Moreover, the Precision of the case of 3 attackers is lower than the cases of 2 and 4 attackers. This is because the cases of 2 attackers and 4 attackers are likely to be mistakenly determined as the case of 3 attackers. In general, our observation indicates that the Hit Rate decreases as the number of attackers increases. However, when the number of attackers increases, the adversaries also increase the probability to expose themselves. In the rest of our study we will only present the results up to 4 attackers that masquerade the same node identity simultaneously.

4.2.2 System Evolution

4.2.2.1 Attacker Number Determination

The System Evolution is a new method to analyze cluster structures and estimate the number of clusters [4]. The System Evolution method uses the *twin-cluster* model, which are the two closest clusters (e.g. clusters a and b) among K potential clusters of a data set. The twin-cluster model is used for energy calculation. The Partition Energy $E_p(K)$ denotes the border distance between the twin clusters, whereas the Merging Energy $E_m(K)$ is calculated as the average distance between elements in the border region of the twin clusters. The border region includes a number of sample points chosen from clusters a and b that are closer to its twin cluster than any other points within its own cluster. For instance, if cluster a contains total M_a sample points, in the twin-cluster model, a will be partitioned into $D_a = \frac{\sqrt{M_a}}{2}$ parts. Then the number of sample points in the border region is defined as $n_a = \frac{M_a}{D_a}$. The same rule is carried out for its twin cluster b. Thus we compute the Partition Energy $E_p(K)$ as:

$$E_p(K) = \frac{1}{n_a + n_b} \{ \sum_{i=1}^{n_a} \min_{j=1,..n_b} D(a_i, b_j)$$

$$+ \sum_{j=1}^{n_b} \min_{i=1,..n_a} D(a_i, b_j) \}, \tag{4.11}$$

and the Merging Energy $E_m(K)$ as:

$$E_m(K) = \frac{1}{\binom{n_a + n_b}{2}} \sum_{i=1}^{(n_a + n_b - 1)} \sum_{j=i+1}^{(n_a + n_b)} D(s_i, s_j), \tag{4.12}$$

Fig. 4.2 System Evolution: detection of 4 adversaries masquerading the same node identity

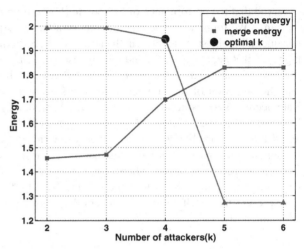

where $D(a_i, b_j)$ is the Euclidean/Pearson distance between the elements a_i and b_j in clusters a and b respectively. And $\mathbf{s}_i, \mathbf{s}_j \in \{a_i\} \bigcup \{b_j\}$, which are the elements in the border region of the twin clusters.

The basic idea behind using the System Evolution method to determine the number of attackers is that all the rest of clusters are separated if the twin clusters are separable. Starting from the initial state with $K = 2$, the algorithm works with PAM by changing the number of clusters in a data set through the partitioning process $E_p(K) > E_m(K)$ and the merging process $E_m(K) \geq E_p(K)$ alternatively.

The algorithm stops when it reaches a equilibrium state $K_{optimal}$, at which the optimal number of clusters is found in the data set: $K_{optimal} = K$, if $E_p(K) > E_m(K)$ and $E_p(K + 1) \leq E_m(K + 1)$.

Figure 4.2 presents an example of using the System Evolution method to determine the number of attackers in the 802.11 network. It shows the energy calculation vs. the number of clusters. The $K_{optimal}$ is obtained when $K = 4$ with $E_p(4) > E_m(4)$ and $E_p(5) < E_m(5)$ indicating that there are 4 adversaries in the network using the same identity to perform spoofing attacks.

4.2.2.2 Experimental Evaluation

In this section, we show our study of System Evolution using multi-class ROC graphs. We perform threshold τ' testing on $E_p(K) - E_m(K)$. We can then obtain the number of attackers $K_{optimal}$ based on: $K_{optimal} = K$, if $E_p(K) - E_m(K) > \tau'$ and $E_p(K + 1) - E_m(K + 1) \leq \tau'$. Figure 4.3 presents the multi-class ROC graphs using both class-reference based method (i.e., the cases of 2 and 4 attackers) and benefit-error based method (i.e., the case of 3 attackers) by varying the threshold τ'. Because of the overall higher Hit Rate under the 802.15.4 network, we only present the results of the 802.11 network in Fig. 4.3. By using the class-reference based method, in Fig. 4.3a and b, we observed better performance of Hit Rate under the

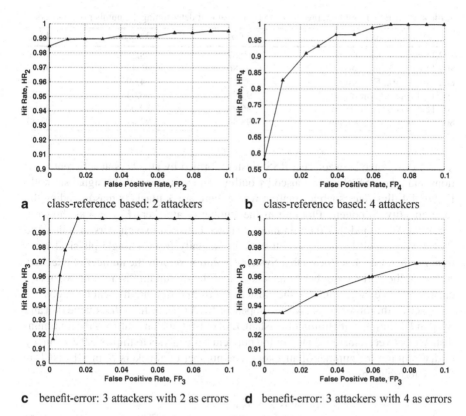

a   class-reference based: 2 attackers   **b**   class-reference based: 4 attackers

c   benefit-error: 3 attackers with 2 as errors   **d**   benefit-error: 3 attackers with 4 as errors

Fig. 4.3 System Evolution in 802.11 network: Multi-class Receiver Operating Characteristic (ROC) Graphs of Hit Rate vs. False Positive

case of 2 attackers than the case of 4 attackers when the False Positive Rate decreases. Turning to examine the ROC graphs of the case of 3 attackers by using the benefit-error based method as shown in Fig. 4.3c and d, we found that bounded by less than 10 % False Positive Rate, the Hit Rate is lower when treating 4 attackers as errors than treating 2 attackers as errors. This indicates that the probability of misclassifying 3 attackers as 4 attackers is higher than that of misclassifying 3 attackers as 2 attackers.

4.2.3 The SILENCE Mechanism

The advantage of Silhouette Plot is that it is suitable for estimating the best partition. Whereas the System Evolution method performs well under difficult cases such as when there exists slightly overlapping between clusters and there are smaller clusters near larger clusters [4]. However, we observed that for both Silhouette Plot and System Evolution methods, the Hit Rate decreases as the number of attackers increases, although the Precision increases. This is because the clustering algorithms can not

Table 4.2 SILENCE: hit rate, precision, and F-measure of determining the number of attackers

Number of attackers	2 (%)	3 (%)	4 (%)
802.11 network, hit rate	99.67	98.21	90.06
802.11 network, precision	98.86	91.42	99.72
802.11 network, F-measure	99.27	94.69	94.64
802.15.4 network, hit rate	99.93	96.04	87.80
802.15.4 network, precision	96.99	89.04	99.96
802.15.4 network, F-measure	98.44	92.41	93.49

tell the difference between real RSS clusters formed by attackers at different positions and fake RSS clusters caused by outliers and variations of the signal strength. Figure 4.4 illustrates such a situation where there are 3 attackers masquerading the same identity. Silhouette Plot returns the number of attackers $K_{sp} = 4$ as shown in Fig. 4.4a. We found that the minimum distance between two clusters in Silhouette Plot is very small because two clusters are actually from a single physical location. Further, Fig. 4.4b shows that System Evolution returns the number of attackers $K_{se} = 3$, the correct number of attackers, and the minimum distance between two clusters is large indicating that the clusters are from different physical locations.

Based on this observation, we developed $SILENCE$, testing SIL houette Plot and System Evolutio$N$ with minimum distanCE of cluster, which evaluates the minimum distance between clusters on top of the pure cluster analysis to improve the accuracy of determining the number of attackers. The number of attackers K in SILENCE is thus determined by:

$$K = \begin{cases} K_{sp} & \text{if } K_{sp} = K_{se}; \\ K_{sp} & \text{if } \min(D_m^{obs})_{K_{sp}} > \min\left(D_m^{obs}\right)_{K_{se}}; \\ K_{se} & \text{if } \min(D_m^{obs})_{K_{sp}} < \min\left(D_m^{obs}\right)_{K_{se}}, \end{cases} \quad (4.13)$$

where D_m^{obs} is the observed value of D_m between two clusters. SILENCE takes the advantage of both Silhouette Plot and System Evolution and further makes the judgment by checking the minimum distance between the returned clusters to make sure the clusters are produced by attackers instead of RSS variations and outliers. Hence, when applying SILENCE to the case shown in Fig. 4.4, SILENCE returns $K = 3$ as the number of attackers, which is the true positive in this example.

4.2.3.1 Experimental Evaluation

The effectiveness of using SILENCE to determine the number of attackers is presented in Table 4.2. And Fig. 4.5 presents the comparison of Hit Rate and F-measure of SILENCE to those of Silhouette Plot and System Evolution methods. The key observation is that there is a significant increase of Hit Rate for all the cases of the number of attackers under study. In particular, for the 802.11 network, the Hit Rate has increased from $89 \sim 92\,\%$ in Silhouette Plot and System Evolution to 98 % using SILENCE for the case of 3 attackers and from $80 \sim 82\,\%$ to 90 % for the 4 attackers

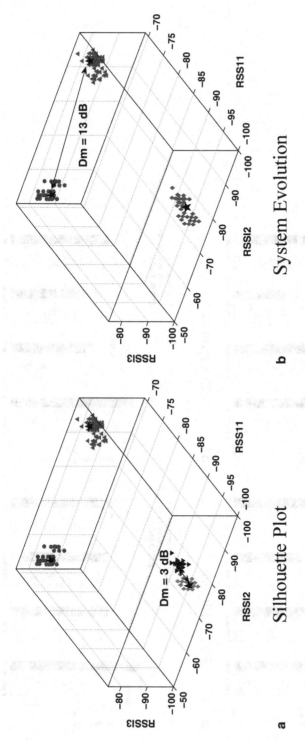

Fig. 4.4 Illustration of the minimum cluster distance using cluster analysis methods under the case of 3 attackers

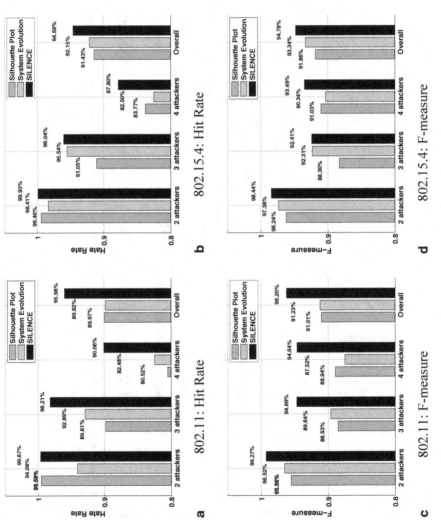

Fig. 4.5 Hit Rate and F-measure comparison of SILENCE to methods using cluster analysis alone such as Silhouette and System Evolution

case. Whereas for the 802.15.4 network, the Hit Rate has increased from around $91 \sim 95\%$ to 96% in SILENCE for the case of 3 attackers and from 84 to 88% for the 4 attackers case. Further, We observed that SILENCE has better performance over all the 2, 3 and 4 attackers in terms of F-measure. The overall improvement of F-measure is from 91 to 96% for 802.11 network, and from $92 \sim 93\%$ to 95% for 802.15.4 network. Further, comparing with Silhouette Plot and System Evolution, the computational cost of SILENCE does not increase much. We experienced that SILENCE can determine the number of attackers within one second for each experimental run. These results demonstrate that SILENCE, a mechanism that combines minimum distance testing and cluster analysis together to perform multiclass attacker detection, is more effective than using techniques based on cluster analysis alone.

4.2.4 Support Vector Machines Based Mechanism

Provided the training data collected during the offline training phase, we can further improve the performance of determining the number of spoofing attackers. In addition, given several statistic methods available to detect the number of attackers, such as the *System Evolution* and *SILENCE*, we can combine the characteristics of these methods to achieve a higher detection rate. In this section, we explore using Support Vector Machines (SVM) to classify the number of the spoofing attackers. The advantage of using SVM is that it can combine the intermediate results (i.e. features) from different statistic methods to build a model based on training data to accurately predict the number of attackers.

Particularly, SVM is a set of kernel based learning methods for data classification, which involves a training phase and a testing phase [5]. Each data instance in the training set consists of a target value (i.e., class label) and several attributes (i.e., features). For example, in our spoofing detection problem, we can use a target value of '+1' to label the result if there are two attackers and a value of '−1' to label the result if the number of attackers is not two. Furthermore, the features can be the difference of the partition energy and merge energy from System Evolution, or the minimum distance between two clusters from SILENCE, or the combination of them. The goal of SVM is to produce a model from the training set to predict the target value of data instances (i.e. the testing data).

Given a training set of instance-label pairs $(x_i; y_i); i = 1, \ldots l$, where $x_i \in R^n$ is the n dimension features and $y_i \in [+1, -1]$ is the label, the support vector machines require the solution of the following optimization problem [5]:

$$\min_{\mathbf{w},b,\xi} \frac{1}{2}\mathbf{w}^T\mathbf{w} + C\sum_{i=1}^{l}\xi_i$$

$$\text{Subject to } y_i\left(\mathbf{w}^T\phi(x_i) + b\right) \geq 1 - \xi_i, \tag{4.14}$$

$$\xi_i \geq 0.$$

Its dual is

$$\min_{\alpha} \frac{1}{2}\alpha^T Q\alpha - \mathbf{e}^T\alpha$$

Subject to $\mathbf{y}^T\alpha = 0,$ (4.15)

$$0 \leq \alpha_i \leq C, i = 1,\dots,l,$$

where $\mathbf{e}$ is the vector of all ones, Q is an l by l positive semidefinite matrix, $Q_{ij} = y_i \cdot y_j \cdot K\left(x_i, x_j\right)$, and $K\left(x_i, x_j\right) \equiv \phi(x_i)^T \phi(x_j)$ is called the kernel function. $C > 0$ is the penalty parameter of the error term. The training vectors x_i are mapped into a higher dimensional space by the function ϕ. SVM then finds a linear separating hyperplane with the maximal margin in that higher dimensional space. Though several kernels are being proposed by researchers, we use the simple linear kernel for our testing [6]:

$$K\left(x_i, x_j\right) = x_i^T x_j. \qquad\qquad (4.16)$$

Furthermore, given a new instance x', the decision function on its label y' is given by:

$$y' = \text{sgn}\left(\sum_{i=1}^{l} y_i\alpha_i K\left(x_i, x'\right) + b\right). \qquad\qquad (4.17)$$

Since the classification of the number of attackers is a multi-class problem, the original binary SVM classifier needs to be extended to a multi-class classifier. In literature, there are many approaches can be used to combine the original binary SVM classifier to k-class classifiers [7], such as *one-against-all* and *one-against-one*. In our testing, we use the *one-against-one* method because it has shorter training time and better performance than *one-against-all* [8]. In the *one-against-one* method, there are $\frac{k(k-1)}{2}$ classifiers constructed, one for each possible class pair. For example, if the possible number of attackers belongs to $\{1, 2, 3, 4\}$, there will be $\frac{4 \times (4-1)}{2}$ classifiers constructed, and each classifier is for one possible class pair, such as $\{1, 3\}$, and etc. The testing instance is first classified by using all the classifiers, where a vote is added for the winning class over each classifier. The class with the most votes will be declared as the final result. Continuing from the above example, if the class 3 obtains the most votes, the number of spoofing attackers is declared as 3.

4.2.4.1 Experimental Evaluation

To validate the effectiveness of the SVM-based mechanism for determining the number of attackers, we randomly choose half of the data as training data, whereas the rest of data for testing. The features we used are the combination of the difference of partition energy and merge energy from System Evolution and the minimum distance between two clusters from SILENCE. Specifically, we used 10-dimension feature, five dimensions from the difference of partition energy and merge energy and the

Table 4.3 SVM: hit rate, precision, and F-measure of determining the number of attackers

Number of attackers	2 (%)	3 (%)	4 (%)
802.11 network, hit rate	99.96	99.07	94.83
802.11 network, precision	99.10	95.65	99.92
802.11 network, F-measure	99.52	97.33	97.31
802.15.4 network, hit rate	99.99	96.49	92.41
802.15.4 network, precision	97.44	92.86	99.99
802.15.4 network, F-measure	98.70	94.64	96.06

other five dimensions from the minimum distance between clusters. That is, we partition the raw data into 2, 3, 4, 5 and 6 clusters, respectively. For each partition, we have one difference of partition energy and merge energy and one minimum distance between clusters. Our goal is to determine how many attackers presented in the raw data.

Table 4.3 shows experimental results of using SVM-based mechanism when the attacker number $i = \{2, 3, 4\}$ for both the 802.11 and the 802.15.4 networks. We observed that the performance of SVM in both networks are similar. We found that when the number of attackers equals to 2, the SVM achieves both the highest Hit Rate, above 99 %, and the highest F-measure value, over 98 %. Moreover, the case of 4 attackers achieves the highest Precision, above 99 %, which indicates that the detection of the number of attackers is highly accurate, however, the Hit Rate decreases to about 90 %.

By comparing the results of SVM to those of Silhouette Plot, System Evolution and SILENCE methods, we found that there is a significant increase of Hit Rate, Precision and F-measure for all the cases of the number of attackers under study. This is due to the facts that the SVM-based mechanism uses the training data to build a prediction model and it also takes the advantages of the combination features from two statistic methods. These results demonstrate that SVM-based mechanism, a classification approach that combines training data and different statistic features is more effective in performing multi-class attacker detection when multiple attackers are present in the system.

4.3 Localizing Adversaries

In this section we present our integrated system that can localize multiple adversaries. The experimental results are presented to evaluate the effectiveness of our approach, especially when attackers using different transmission power levels.

4.3.1 Framework

The traditional localization approaches are based on averaged RSS from each node identity inputs to estimate the position of a node. However, in wireless spoofing attacks, the RSS stream of a node identity may be mixed with RSS readings of both the original node as well as spoofing nodes from different physical locations. The traditional method of averaging RSS readings cannot differentiate RSS readings from different locations and thus is not feasible for localizing adversaries.

Different from traditional localization approaches, our integrated detection and localization system utilizes the RSS medoids returned from attack detection algorithm as inputs to localization algorithms to estimate the positions of adversaries. The return positions from our system includes the location estimate of the original node and the attackers in the physical space.

Handling Adversaries Using Different Transmission Power Levels An adversary may vary the transmission power levels when performing spoofing attacks so that the localization system cannot estimate its location accurately. We examine the pass loss equation that models the received power as a function of the distance to the landmark:

$$P(d)[dBm] = P(d_0)[dBm] - 10\gamma \log_{10}\left(\frac{d}{d_0}\right), \tag{4.18}$$

where $P(d_0)$ represents the transmitting power of a node at the reference distance d_0, d is the distance between the transmitting node and the landmark, and γ is the path loss exponent. Further, we can express the difference of the received power between two landmarks, i and j, as:

$$P(d_i) - P(d_j) = 10\gamma_i \log_{10}\left(\frac{d_i}{d_0}\right) - 10\gamma_j \log_{10}\left(\frac{d_j}{d_0}\right). \tag{4.19}$$

Based on Eq. (4.19), we found that the difference of the corresponding received power between two different landmarks is independent of the transmission power levels. Thus, when an adversary residing at a physical location varies its transmission power to perform a spoofing attack, the difference of the RSS readings between two different landmarks from the adversary is a constant since the RSS readings are obtained from a single physical location. We can then utilize the difference of the medoids vectors in signal space obtained from attack detection algorithm to localize adversaries.

4.3.2 Algorithms

In order to evaluate the generality of our integrated localization system for localizing adversaries, we have chosen a set of representative localization algorithms ranging from nearest neighbor matching in signal space (RADAR [9]), to probability-based (Area-Based Probability [10]), and to multilateration (Bayesian Networks [11]).

RADAR-Gridded The RADAR-Gridded algorithm is a scene-matching localization algorithm extended from [9]. RADAR-Gridded uses an interpolated signal map, which is built from a set of averaged RSS readings with known (x, y) locations. Given an observed RSS reading with an unknown location, RADAR returns the x,

Fig. 4.6 Bayesian graphical
model in our study

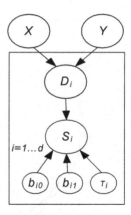

y of the nearest neighbor in the signal map to the one to localize, where "nearest" is
defined as the Euclidean distance of RSS points in an N-dimensional signal space,
where N is the number of landmarks.

Area Based Probability (ABP) ABP also utilizes an interpolated signal map [10].
Further, the experimental area is divided into a regular grid of equal sized tiles. ABP
assumes the distribution of RSS for each landmark follows a Gaussian distribution
with mean as the expected value of RSS reading vector $\mathbf{s}$. ABP then computes the
probability of the wireless device being at each tile L_i, with $i = 1 \ldots L$, on the floor
using Bayes' rule:

$$P(L_i|\mathbf{s}) = \frac{P(\mathbf{s}|L_i) \times P(L_i)}{P(\mathbf{s})} \qquad (4.20)$$

Given that the wireless node must be at exactly one tile satisfying $\sum_{i=1}^{L} P(L_i|\mathbf{s}) = 1$,
ABP normalizes the probability and returns the most likely tiles/grids up to its
confidence α.

Bayesian Networks (BN) BN localization is a multilateration algorithm that en-
codes the signal-to-distance propagation model into the Bayesian Graphical Model
for localization [11]. Figure 4.6 shows the basic Bayesian Network used for our
study. The vertices X and Y represent location; the vertex s_i is the RSS reading from
the ith landmark; and the vertex D_i represents the Euclidean distance between the
location specified by X and Y and the ith landmark. The value of s_i follows a signal
propagation model $s_i = b_{0i} + b_{1i} \log D_i$, where b_{0i}, b_{1i} are the parameters specific to
the ith landmark. The distance $D_i = \sqrt{(X - x_i)^2 + (Y - y_i)^2}$ in turn depends on the
location (X, Y) of the measured signal and the coordinates (x_i, y_i) of the ith landmark.
The network models noise and outliers by modeling the s_i as a Gaussian distribution
around the above propagation model, with variance τ_i: $s_i \sim N(b_{0i} + b_{1i} \log D_i, \tau_i)$.
Through Markov Chain Monte Carlo (MCMC) simulation, BN returns the sampling
distribution of the possible location of X and Y as the localization result.

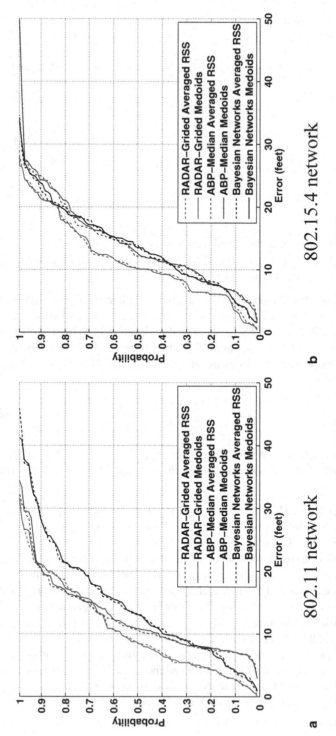

Fig. 4.7 Comparison of localization errors between using medoids from cluster analysis and using averaged RSS

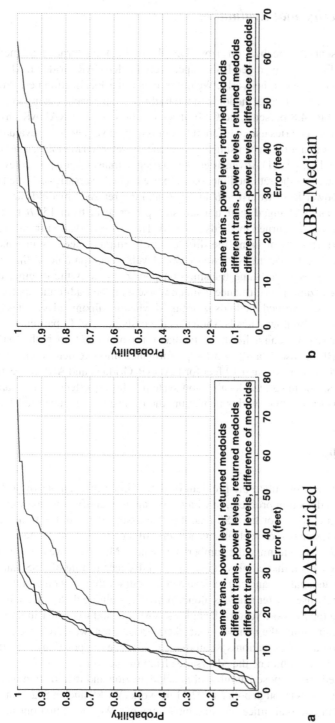

Fig. 4.8 Localization errors when adversaries using different transmission power levels

4.3.3 Experimental Evaluation

Figure 4.7 presents the localization error CDF when using the returned RSS medoids from SILENCE and the averaged RSS respectively for RADAR-Gridded, ABP, and Bayesian Networks in two networks. We observed similar localization performance when using the returned RSS medoids to the traditional approaches using averaged RSS. Further, Fig. 4.8 presents the CDF of localization error of RADAR-Gridded and ABP when adversaries using different transmission power levels. To evaluate the performance of our approach by using the difference of returned medoids, three cases are presented in Fig. 4.8: (1) Adversaries used the same transmission power levels as the original node and the returned medoids are used; (2) Adversaries changed their transmission power level from $15dB$ to $10dB$ and the returned medoids are used; and (3) Adversaries changed their transmission power level from $15dB$ to $10dB$ and the difference of returned medoids are used. The key observation from Fig. 4.8 is that the performance of using the difference of returned medoids in handling adversaries using different transmission power levels is comparable to the results when adversaries used the same transmission power levels as the original node. Further, the localization performance is much worse than the traditional approaches if the difference of returned medoids is not used when localizing adversaries using different transmission power levels, shown as the case 2 above. In particular, when using our approach we can achieve the median error of 13 feet for both RADAR-Grided and ABP in case 3, a $40 \sim 50\%$ performance improvement, comparing to the median errors of 20 feet and 19 feet for RADAR-Gridded and ABP respectively in case 2. Thus, our integrated localization system is highly effective in localizing multiple adversaries with or without changing their transmission power levels.

4.4 Summary

In this chapter, we formulate the problem of determining the number of attackers as a multi-class detection problem, in which we want to identify how many clusters exist in the signal space for the RSS readings that associated with the same device identity. Two cluster-based mechanisms, namely Silhouette Plot and System Evolution, are proposed to determine the number of attackers. Moreover, we developed the SILENCE mechanism that employs the minimum distance testing of RSS values in addition to cluster analysis and can achieve better accuracy than other methods under study that merely use cluster analysis alone. When the training data is available, we explored using the Support Vector Machines (SVM) method to further improve the accuracy of determining the number of attackers. In addition, we developed an integrated detection and localization system that can localize the positions of multiple attackers in order to eliminate the adversaries from the network.

We evaluated our proposed number of attack detection and localization methods by using two testbeds through both an 802.11 network (Wi-Fi) and an 802.15.4 (Zig-Bee) network in two real office building environments. We found that our number of adversaries detection methods achieves over 90 % hit rates and precision simultaneously when using SILENCE and SVM-based mechanism. Further, based on the number of attackers determined by our mechanisms, our integrated detection and localization system can localize any number of adversaries even when attackers using different transmission power levels. The performance of localizing adversaries achieves similar results as those under normal conditions, thereby, providing strong evidence of the effectiveness of our approach in detecting wireless spoofing attacks, determining the number of attackers and localizing adversaries.

References

1. C. van Rijsbergen, *Information Retrieval, Second Edition*. Butterworths, 1979.
2. T. Fawcett, "An introduction to ROC analysis," *Pattern Recognition Letters, Elsevier*, vol. 27, pp. 861–874, 2006.
3. P. Rousseeuw, "Silhouettes: a graphical aid to the interpretation and validation of cluster analysis," *Journal of Computational and Applied Mathematics*, vol. 20, no. 1, pp. 53–65, November 1987.
4. K. Wang, J. Zheng, J. Zhang, and J. Dong, "Estimating the number of clusters via system evolution for cluster analysis of gene expression data," *IEEE Transactions on Information Technology in Biomedicine*, vol. 13, no. 5, pp. 848–853, 2009.
5. N. Cristianini and J. Shawe-Taylor, *An introduction to support Vector Machines: and other kernel-based learning methods*. Cambridge Univ Pr, 2000.
6. C.-C. Chang and C.-J. Lin, *LIBSVM: a library for support vector machines*, 2001, software available at http://www.csie.ntu.edu.tw/~cjlin/libsvm.
7. V. Franc and V. Hlaváč, "Multi-class support vector machine," in *International Conference on Pattern Recognition*, vol. 16, 2002, pp. 236–239.
8. C. Hsu and C. Lin, "A comparison of methods for multiclass support vector machines," *IEEE transactions on Neural Networks*, vol. 13, no. 2, pp. 415–425, 2002.
9. P. Bahl and V. N. Padmanabhan, "RADAR: An in-building RF-based user location and tracking system," in *Proceedings of the IEEE International Conference on Computer Communications (INFOCOM)*, March 2000, pp. 775–784.
10. E. Elnahrawy, X. Li, and R. P. Martin, "The limits of localization using signal strength: A comparative study," in *Proceedings of the First IEEE International Conference on Sensor and Ad hoc Communcations and Networks (SECON 2004)*, Oct. 2004, pp. 406–414.
11. D. Madigan, E. Elnahrawy, R. Martin, W. Ju, P. Krishnan, and A. S. Krishnakumar, "Bayesian indoor positioning systems," in *Proceedings of the IEEE International Conference on Computer Communications (INFOCOM)*, March 2005, pp. 324–331.

Chapter 5
Detecting Mobile Agents Using Identity Fraud

5.1 Motivation

Attacks involving identity fraud can facilitate a variety of advanced attacks to significantly impact the normal operation of wireless networks [1–4]. Identity fraud performed by mobile wireless devices may further inflict security and privacy damages on the social life of the individual who carries wireless devices. We call these kind of attacks as *mobile spoofing attacks*. There has been active work in detecting spoofing attacks [3, 5, 6]. [3] proposed the use of matching rules of Received Signal Strength (RSS) for spoofing detection, [5] used K-means cluster analysis of RSS, and [6] modeled RSS readings as a Gaussian mixture model to capture antenna diversity. However, these mechanisms only work in static wireless environments, i.e., the victim node has a fixed location. In this chapter, we focus on spoofing attack detection in mobile wireless environments, that is, the wireless devices including the victim node and/or the spoofing node are moving around. Thus, detecting identity fraud launched by mobile agents is important as it allows the network to further exploit a wide range of defense strategies in different network layers, and consequently helps to ensure secure and trustworthy communication in emerging mobile pervasive computing.

We propose a system called DEMOTE, *de*tecting *mo*bile spoofing a*t*tacks in wireless environments, which exploits the correlation within the RSS trace based on each node's identity to perform attack detection in either the signal space or the physical space. DEMOTE utilizes an unsupervised thresholding approach to find an optimal threshold to partition the RSS trace of a node identity into two classes. Given the RSS is distinctively correlated to a wireless node's physical location, the partitioned two classes will be highly correlated if there is no spoofing attacks, whereas less or not correlated when a spoofing attack is present.

The key challenge in DEMOTE is to reconstruct the RSS trace based on the partitioned classes that belong to different physical nodes accurately when a spoofing attack is occurring. Although we are lack of knowledge of knowing the spatial constraint of mobile wireless nodes, we found that there is a temporal constraint that is unique to the RSS trace from each physical node. We developed a simple algorithm, ALignment Prediction (ALP), which utilizes the characteristic of the temporal constraint and predicts the most possible RSS value in the next time slot for accurate trace reconstruction over time.

J. Yang et al., *Pervasive Wireless Environments: Detecting and Localizing User Spoofing*, SpringerBriefs in Computer Science, DOI 10.1007/978-3-319-07356-9_5, © The Author(s) 2014

To validate our approach, we conducted experiments in an office building environment across different technologies including IEEE 802.11 b/g and IEEE 802.15.4. We deployed our own traffic sniffers or utilized the existing Access Points (APs) at fixed locations to collect RSS packets of mobile devices. Our experimental results show that DEMOTE is highly effective in detecting spoofing attacks in mobile environments by using only one AP in the signal space. Further, if the localization process is conducted, DEMOTE can detect spoofing attacks by using the physical position estimates obtained from localization based on multiple APs.

The rest of the chapter is organized as follows. In Sect. 5.2, we specify the attack model and present the theoretical approach used in the DEMOTE system. We describe our experimental methodology and present the validation results across different wireless technologies in Sect. 5.3. Finally, we conclude in Sect. 5.4.

5.2   Detection System Approach

5.2.1   Attack Model

In this work, rather than considering that the victim nodes are static, we focus on the situation when the victim nodes are mobile. We consider the spoofing nodes to be either mobile or static. When both the victim node and the spoofing node are static, spoofing attacks can be detected by using the techniques in previous works [4–6]. For detecting the mobility of wireless devices, we can use existing metrics, such as the variance of RSS and the techniques presented in [7–9]. Thus it is possible to distinguish the mobile nodes from the static nodes in wireless networks.

We deploy traffic observers or use the Access Points (APs) directly that are at fixed locations to record the Received Signal Strength of packets in the network. When a spoofing attack is conducted, we assume that the victim node, whose identity is cloned by the adversary, is also present in the network. In addition, when the attacker is moving around, we assume that the attacker is not moving together with the victim node, which means that the victim node and the spoofing node have different movement patterns. It is a reasonable assumption because it requires bigger efforts for an attacker to move together with the victim node by tracing the victim node in all the time intervals. In addition, if the spoofing device is co-moving with the victim node, the attacker also increases the possibility of exposing itself to the victim node. We note that under the case that the spoofing attack is present in a different network region of the victim node, a high-level domain management server should be able to detect the attack since the same node identity has appeared in more than one networks.

5.2.2   DEMOTE System Overview

DEMOTE performs spoofing attack detection by analyzing the RSS trace for each mobile node identity. RSS is widely available in wireless communication networks and governed by the distance from a device to an AP. This implies that RSS readings are highly correlated with the physical location of a wireless device [5], and thus RSS readings represent a means to distinguish between devices as they move around an environment.

The main idea of the DEMOTE technique is to use the relationship between the RSS and the physical location of a mobile device to perform spoofing attacks detection. If a spoofing attack is present, the RSS trace from *claimed* node identity is the mixture of two RSS traces: one belongs to the victim node and the other belongs to the spoofing node. These two RSS traces are correlated to the different locations of the two physical nodes and are thus not highly correlated to each other. Under normal situations, i.e., there is no spoofing attacks present, the RSS trace from one node identity belongs to one physical node. If the RSS trace is separated into two traces, those two traces are highly correlated to each other as they are determined by the movement pattern of a single mobile node.

To obtain a high detection rate, the key challenge in DEMOTE is to accurately partition and reconstruct the RSS trace that belongs to different physical nodes under a spoofing attack. When the nodes are static, the RSS readings are usually modeled as a Gaussian distribution [10]. The mixed RSS readings from two different nodes can then be modeled as two mixed Gaussian distribution and they can be separated by using the method of Gaussian mixture models [11]. However, when a wireless device is moving around, the distribution of RSS readings is highly dependent on the movement pattern of the node, such as the speed and the direction of the wireless node. Further, it is prohibitive to derive a closed form distribution of RSS trace even with the knowledge of the movement pattern of the wireless node.

Thus, instead of trying to model the RSS readings as any estimated distribution, DEMOTE utilizes an unsupervised thresholding approach to achieve an optimal threshold when performing trace partitioning and separates the RSS readings into two classes. Further, from the two partitioned classes, in order to reconstruct the two RSS traces that belong to two different physical nodes under a spoofing attack or one physical node under a normal situation, we develop the ALignment Prediction (ALP) algorithm that makes use of the temporal constraints inherited from the RSS readings over time, which result from assumptions on the speed and continuity of a mobile device's movement, and helps to predict the most probable RSS value for the next time interval. Finally, DEMOTE computes the correlation coefficients either of the two reconstructed RSS traces in the signal space or of the localization estimates in the physical space based on these two traces. Under a spoofing attack, the two RSS traces come from two different physical devices and thus the value of the correlation coefficient should be low. DEMOTE contains three components: *RSS Partitioning*, *Trace Reconstruction* and *Correlation Coefficient Calculation*. The system flow of DEMOTE is shown in Fig. 5.1. In the following, we describe the theoretic approach of each component in DEMOTE.

5.2.3 RSS Partitioning

Suppose the RSS trace from one node identity within time window T of a single AP is S. We equally divide the trace S into n non overlapping time intervals. Let the

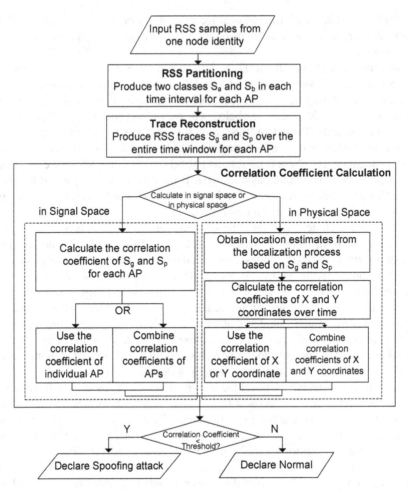

Fig. 5.1 System flow of DEMOTE

RSS readings in the ith time interval be denoted as S_i. Then, S can be represented as $\{S_1, S_2 \ldots, S_n\}$. The objective of the *RSS Partitioning* component is to partition the RSS readings within one time interval, S_i into two classes S_{ai} and S_{bi}, one belongs to the victim node and the other belongs to the spoofing node under a spoofing attack. In this subsection, we first analyze how to obtain the optimal threshold that can minimize the partitioning error of the RSS readings. We then describe a nonparametric and unsupervised method to obtain the optimal threshold for RSS partitioning in DEMOTE.

5.2.3.1 Optimal Thresholding

Let s denote the random variable governing the RSS readings. Suppose the probability density function (PDF) of S_i is $p(s)$. Under a spoofing attack, the density function

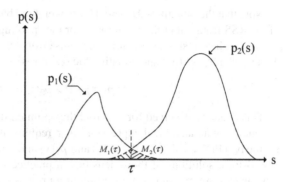

Fig. 5.2 RSS probability density functions of two classes

$p(s)$ is the mixture of two probability densities, one for the victim node and the other for the spoofing node as illustrated in Fig. 5.2. Whereas under a normal situation, $p(s)$ is the probability density of a legitimate node. If the form of the densities is known, it is possible to determine an optimal threshold for partitioning the mixture of RSS into two classes in terms of minimum partition error.

Figure 5.2 shows two probability density functions, the left side one $p_1(s)$ describes the RSS of victim node, while the right side one $p_2(s)$ corresponds to the spoofing node. Then, the mixture PDF describing the overall RSS variation is

$$p(s) = P_{r1}p_1(s) + P_{r2}p_2(s), \tag{5.1}$$

where P_{r1} and P_{r2} are the probabilities of occurrence of two classes of RSS values respectively. Since any given RSS value either belongs to the victim node or to the spoofing node, we have

$$P_{r1} + P_{r2} = 1. \tag{5.2}$$

Now, our objective is to select the value of threshold τ that minimizes the average error in making the decisions that a given RSS belongs to the victim node or the spoofing node. Thus, the probability of erroneously classifying a spoofing node's RSS as a victim node's RSS is

$$M_1(\tau) = \int_{-\infty}^{\tau} p_2(s)ds. \tag{5.3}$$

This is the area under the curve of $p_2(s)$ to the left of the threshold. Similarly, the probability of erroneously classifying a victim node's RSS as a spoofing node's RSS is

$$M_2(\tau) = \int_{\tau}^{+\infty} p_1(s)ds, \tag{5.4}$$

which is the area under the curve of $p_1(s)$ to the right of τ. Then the overall probability of partition error is

$$M(\tau) = P_{r2}M_1(\tau) + P_{r1}M_2(\tau). \tag{5.5}$$

Note that the quantities M_1 and M_2 are weighted by the probability of occurrence of the RSS from either the victim node or the spoofing node.

To find the threshold value for which this error is minimal requires differentiating $M(\tau)$ with respect to τ and equating the result to 0:

$$P_{r1} p_1(\tau) - P_{r2} p_2(\tau) = 0. \tag{5.6}$$

This equation is solved for τ to find the optimum threshold.

Obtaining an analytical expression for τ requires that we know the distributions for the two PDFs which are the $p_1(s)$ and $p_2(s)$ in Eq. (5.6) [12]. However, obtaining closed-form solutions of these densities in practice is not feasible when the wireless devices are moving around. Without a priori knowledge on the distribution of each node's RSS distribution, we obtain an optimal threshold by applying the *Otsu* method [13].

5.2.3.2 Trace Partitioning Approach

We sort RSS values in S_i for the ith time interval. The distinct RSS values are denoted as s_j with $j \in \{1, 2 \ldots, L\}$ and L is the number of distinctive values in S_i. Further, the number of RSS samples whose value is s_j is denoted as n_j and the total number of RSS is $N = n_1 + n_2 + \ldots + n_L$ within the ith time interval. Then the probability distribution of each value can be denoted by

$$p(s_j) = \frac{n_j}{N}, \quad \text{with} \quad p(s_j) \geq 0, \sum_{j=1}^{L} p(s_j) = 1. \tag{5.7}$$

Under a spoofing attack, s_j can either belong to the RSS class of the victim node or belong to the RSS class of the spoofing node. The values of these two RSS classes usually have overlaps. We use the Otsu method, which uses the discriminate criterion [14] to choose the optimal threshold, in order to make the partitioned classes as tight as possible and thus minimize their overlap. The search criteria for the optimal threshold τ is the minimization of the weighted sum of the variances of two classes (i.e. within-class variance):

$$\delta_w^2(\tau) = P_{r1}(\tau)\delta_1^2(\tau) + P_{r2}(\tau)\delta_2^2(\tau), \tag{5.8}$$

where $P_{r1}(\tau) = \sum_{j=1}^{(\tau-1)} p(s_j)$, $P_{r2}(\tau) = \sum_{j=\tau}^{L} p(s_j)$ are the probabilities of two classes separated by a threshold τ and $\delta_m^2(\tau)(m = 1, 2)$ is the RSS variance in each class.

To reduce the computational complexity of calculating the within-class variance for each possible threshold when searching for the optimal threshold, we subtract the within-class variance from the variance of the mixture of RSS. We then obtain the between-class variance:

$$\begin{aligned}
\delta_b^2(\tau) &= \delta^2 - \delta_w^2(\tau) \\
&= P_{r1}(\tau)[\mu_1(\tau) - \mu]^2 + P_{r2}(\tau)[\mu_2(\tau) - \mu]^2, \tag{5.9}
\end{aligned}$$

where δ^2 is the variance of the mixture of RSS, μ is the mean value of RSS samples in S_i and $\mu_m (m = 1, 2)$ is the mean of each class. Note that $\mu = P_{r1}(\tau)\mu_1(\tau) + P_{r2}(\tau)\mu_2(\tau)$. Substituting μ and simplifying, we get the between-class variance:

$$\delta_b^2(\tau) = P_{r1}(\tau)P_{r2}(\tau)[\mu_1(\tau) - \mu_2(\tau)]^2. \tag{5.10}$$

Thus, the problem of minimizing the within-class variance is simplified and transferred to maximizing the between-class variance, which utilizes only the zeroth- and the first-order cumulative moments of the RSS value histogram. Further, by using simple recurrence relation we can update the between-class variance as we successively test each threshold:

$$P_{r1}(\tau + 1) = P_{r1}(\tau) + p(\tau) \tag{5.11}$$

$$P_{r2}(\tau + 1) = P_{r2}(\tau) - p(\tau) \tag{5.12}$$

$$\mu_1(\tau + 1) = \frac{\mu_1(\tau)P_{r1}(\tau) + p(\tau)\tau}{P_{r1}(\tau + 1)} \tag{5.13}$$

$$\mu_2(\tau + 1) = \frac{\mu_2(\tau)P_{r2}(\tau) - p(\tau)\tau}{P_{r2}(\tau + 1)} \tag{5.14}$$

Compared with other unsupervised thresholding methods such as K-means, the Otsu optimal threshold approach is more accurate in when partitioning two classes. Since K-means just measures distances between RSS samples and centroids of classes, while Otsu also takes care of obtaining compact clusters using the inter-class variance [15].

5.2.4 Trace Reconstruction

From the RSS Partitioning component, we obtained two RSS classes in each time interval, one belongs to the victim node and the other belongs to the spoofing node under a spoofing attack. For spoofing detection, we further need to reconstruct two RSS traces that are associated with two different nodes respectively over the whole time window T. Thus, the objective of the Trace Reconstruction component is to reconstruct two RSS traces, $S_g = \{s_{gi}\}$ and $S_p = \{s_{pi}\}$ in the time window T such that one trace is associated with the victim node and the other associated with the spoofing node.

Based on the partitioned two classes: S_{ai} and S_{bi} for each time interval, since the time interval is small, we can simply use the average value of RSS of each class in a time interval, represented as $\bar{s}_{ai}$ and $\bar{s}_{bi}$ respectively, for trace reconstruction in T. Then in the ith time interval, trace reconstruction needs to determine whether to assign $\bar{s}_{ai}$ to s_{gi} and $\bar{s}_{bi}$ to s_{pi} or the other way around.

Since we don't have a priori knowledge of the movement patterns of wireless devices, we cannot apply spatial constraint when constructing the RSS trace of a moving node. However, there is a temporal constraint presented in the RSS trace, that is, the RSS samples in the consecutive time intervals are correlated. Thus, although the RSS trace in the whole time window T may not follow any form of curve in practice, the RSS trace within several small time intervals can be modeled to follow a conic curve [16]. In the ith time interval, we can use the RSS values of s_{gi} and s_{pi} to predict the RSS values in the $(i + 1)^{th}$ time interval using conic curve fitting. We then compare the predicted values with $\bar{s}_{a(i+1)}$ and $\bar{s}_{b(i+1)}$, and decide how to assign $\bar{s}_{a(i+1)}$ and $\bar{s}_{b(i+1)}$ to $s_{g(i+1)}$ and $s_{p(i+1)}$.

We developed the ALignment Prediction (ALP) algorithm to predict the RSS values during the trace reconstruction. ALP uses the determined RSS values in the last K time intervals ranging from i^{th} to $(i - K - 1)^{th}$ time intervals to perform conic curve fitting and predict the RSS values, $s^p_{g(i+1)}$ and $s^p_{p(i+1)}$, in the $(i + 1)^{th}$ time interval:

$$s^p_{g(i+1)} = a_{g0i} + a_{g1i}(i + 1) + a_{g2i}(i + 1)^2, \tag{5.15}$$

and

$$s^p_{p(i+1)} = a_{p0i} + a_{p1i}(i + 1) + a_{p2i}(i + 1)^2, \tag{5.16}$$

where the coefficients $\{a_{g0i}, a_{g1i}, a_{g2i}\}$ and $\{a_{p0i}, a_{p1i}, a_{p2i}\}$ are determined by the latest K values $\{s_{gi}, s_{g(i-1)}, \ldots, s_{g(i-K-1)}\}$ and $\{s_{pi}, s_{p(i-1)}, \ldots, s_{p(i-K-1)}\}$ according to the Least-squares polynomial approximation [16]. K is an adjustable variable. In our study, we set $K = 4$. We further define the prediction error as

$$P_{e1} = (s^p_{g(i+1)} - \bar{s}_{a(i+1)})^2 + (s^p_{p(i+1)} - \bar{s}_{b(i+1)})^2, \tag{5.17}$$

and

$$P_{e2} = (s^p_{g(i+1)} - \bar{s}_{b(i+1)})^2 + (s^p_{p(i+1)} - \bar{s}_{a(i+1)})^2. \tag{5.18}$$

If $P_{e1} \leq P_{e2}$, we assign $\bar{s}_{a(i+1)}$ to $s_{g(i+1)}$ and $\bar{s}_{b(i+1)}$ to $s_{p(i+1)}$. Otherwise, we assign $\bar{s}_{b(i+1)}$ to $s_{g(i+1)}$ and $\bar{s}_{a(i+1)}$ to $s_{p(i+1)}$.

In the initial setup, when $i = 1$, we set $s_{g1} = \bar{s}_{a1}$, $s_{p1} = \bar{s}_{b1}$ and $s^p_{g2} = s_{g1}$, $s^p_{p2} = s_{p1}$. When $1 < i < K$, we use the first i values of s_{gi} and s_{pi} to fit conic curves and then predict and determine the $(i + 1)^{th}$ RSS value.

The pseudo code of the ALP algorithm is shown in Algorithm 1.

5.2.5 Correlation Coefficient Calculation

Once the RSS traces are reconstructed, intuitively we can calculate the distance between two nodes either in the signal space or in the physical space to detect spoofing. However, due to the high variance of RSS that is caused

---

Algorithm 1 The ALP algorithm

Input: $\{\bar{s}_{ai}\}$ and $\{\bar{s}_{bi}\}$ with $i = \{1, 2 \ldots n\}$, K;
Output: $\{s_{gi}\}$ and $\{s_{pi}\}$ with $i = \{1, 2 \ldots n\}$;
Initialize: Set $s_{g1} = \bar{s}_{a1}$, $s_{p1} = \bar{s}_{b1}$, $s_{g2}^p = s_{g1}$ and $s_{p2}^p = s_{p1}$;
for $i = 2$ to n **do**
    // Calculate prediction errors P_{e1} and P_{e2};
    $P_{e1} = (s_{gi}^p - \bar{s}_{ai})^2 + (s_{pi}^p - \bar{s}_{bi})^2$;
    $P_{e2} = (s_{gi}^p - \bar{s}_{bi})^2 + (s_{pi}^p - \bar{s}_{ai})^2$;
    // Assign $\bar{s}_{ai}, \bar{s}_{bi}$ to s_{gi} and s_{pi} according to prediction errors;
    if $P_{e1} \leq P_{e2}$ **then**
        $s_{gi} = \bar{s}_{ai}, s_{pi} = \bar{s}_{bi}$;
    else
        $s_{gi} = \bar{s}_{bi}, s_{pi} = \bar{s}_{ai}$;
    end if
    // Calculate coefficients of conic curves;
    if $(i < K)$ **then**
        Obtain $\{a_{g0i}, a_{g1i}, a_{g2i}\}$ and $\{a_{p0i}, a_{p1i}, a_{p2i}\}$ using the first i values of $\{s_{gi}\}$ and $\{s_{pi}\}$;
    else
        Obtain $\{a_{g0i}, a_{g1i}, a_{g2i}\}$ and $\{a_{p0i}, a_{p1i}, a_{p2i}\}$ using the latest K values of $\{s_{gi}\}$ and $\{s_{pi}\}$;
    end if
    // Calculate prediction value $s_{g(i+1)}^p$ and $s_{p(i+1)}^p$ for $(i+1)^{th}$ interval;
    $s_{g(i+1)}^p = a_{g0i} + a_{g1i}(i+1) + a_{g2i}(i+1)^2$;
    $s_{p(i+1)}^p = a_{p0i} + a_{p1i}(i+1) + a_{p2i}(i+1)^2$;
end for

---

by random noise, environmental bias, and multipath effects [17]. It is not feasible to derive a threshold and distinguish the normal situation from the attack situation most of the time as illustrated in Fig. 5.3. We thus turn to examine the correlation coefficient of the two RSS traces.

Correlation Coefficient The correlation coefficient measures the degree of linear relationship between two random variables [18]. Instead of calculating the absolute difference of two random variables, the correlation coefficient captures similarities in the changes of two values of random variables. Thus, the correlation coefficient is suitable in determining whether two RSS traces are correlated or not in both signal space and physical space. DEMOTE uses the *Pearson correlation coefficient* [19] to measure the degree of linear relationship between two partitioned traces or their localization results. Given a series of n measurements for random variables X and Y, written as x_i and y_i, where $i = 1, 2, \ldots, n$, the Pearson correlation coefficient of X and Y is written:

$$r_{xy} = \frac{\sum_{i=1}^{n} (x_i - \bar{x})(y_i - \bar{y})}{(n-1)\delta_x \delta_y}, \tag{5.19}$$

where $\bar{x}$ and $\bar{y}$ are the sample means of X and Y, δ_x and δ_y are the sample standard deviations of X and Y. The r_{xy} value ranges from -1 to +1. A value of r_{xy} near +1 or -1 indicates a high degree of linearity between X and Y, whereas a value near 0 indicates a lack of such linearity. A positive value indicates that X and Y tend to change together (i.e. decreasing or increasing), whereas a negative value indicates that Y tends to decrease when X increases.

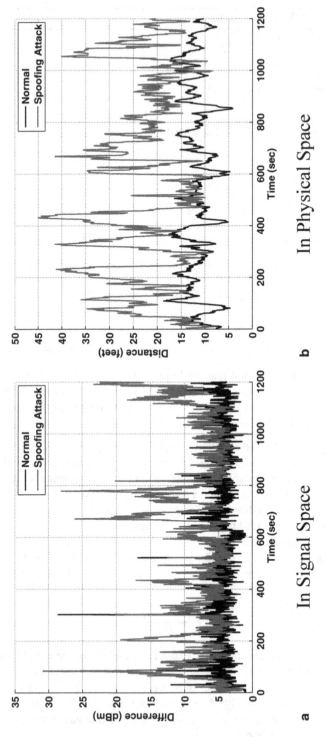

Fig. 5.3 The RSS distance in the signal space and the position distance in the physical space when using the reconstructed RSS traces for spoofing detection

Signal Space When examining the correlation coefficient in signal space, the random variables X and Y correspond to the constructed RSS traces S_g and S_p. Under normal situations, these two RSS traces should be highly correlated since they are from one mobile wireless node and determined by the same movement pattern of the node. However, under a spoofing attack, these two RSS traces are uncorrelated as they come from two different mobile nodes and determined by the movement pattern of each node separately.

Physical Space We further study the correlation coefficient in physical space. We can conduct localization [10] to perform location estimation utilizing the two separated RSS traces. The random variables X and Y then correspond to the localization estimates obtained. Under a normal (non-attack) situation, the localization results obtained in physical space are correlated and directly reflect the movement pattern of the wireless node, whereas they are uncorrelated under a spoofing attacks as the movement patterns of the victim node and the spoofing node are different.

Therefore, by examining the degree of correlation of the RSS traces in either signal space or in physical space, we can determine whether there is spoofing attack present in the network.

5.3 Experimental Evaluation

In this section, we first describe our experimental methodology and metrics that we use to evaluate our approach. We then present the experiment results of detecting mobile spoofing attacks.

5.3.1 Experimental Methodology

5.3.1.1 Experimental Setup

To evaluate the effectiveness of DEMOTE, we conducted experiments using both an 802.11 (Wi-Fi) network as well as an 802.15.4 (ZigBee) network in the Wireless Network Laboratory (WINLAB) at Rutgers University. Figure 5.4 depicts the layout of experiment site, where the floor size is $219 \times 169\,ft$. All experiments were conducted in the yellow shaded area, which is the WINLAB space. We deployed four Access Points (APs) which were used to observe packet traffic at fixed locations in our experiment. Each access point is shown as a red star in Fig. 5.4 and denoted as A, B, C and D. For the 802.11 (Wi-Fi) network, each access point is a Linux machine with a 1-GHz CPU, 512 MBs of RAM and a 20-GB disk. We used Atheros miniPCI 802.11 wireless card, which connected to an external 7 dBi Omni directional antenna to monitor packet traffic. Whereas for the 802.15.4 (ZigBee) network, we attached a Tmote Sky mote on each access point, which is used in 802.11 (Wi-Fi) network, and each Tmote Sky mote connected to an external 7 dBi Omni directional antenna. We configured each attached mote as an access point to monitor the traffic of the 802.15.4 (ZigBee) network.

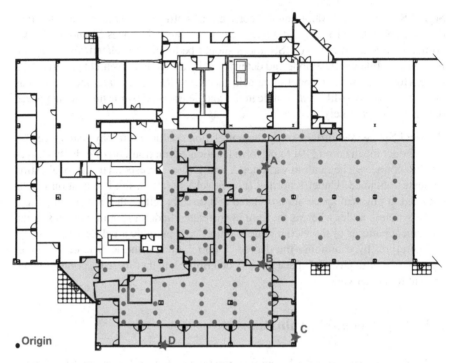

Fig. 5.4 Layout of the experiment floor and the deployment of access points

To collect RSS traces over time, two people carried one laptop each with a Tmote Sky mote attached to the laptop. During the experiment, these two people either stood or randomly walked around. The experiment was one-hour long and each walking/standing period was ten-minutes long. The walking speed was about 4ft/sec (i.e. normal human walking speed) in the yellow shaded area in Fig. 5.4. The laptops transmitted packets at the rate of 10 packets/sec. Each access point recorded the transmitter's MAC address (for Wi-Fi) or ID (for ZigBee), RSS and timestamp of each packet transmitted from the mobile laptops, and then forwarded to a central server to store. We choose one transmitter as the victim node and the other transmitter as the spoofing attacker. Using this experimental setup, when the victim node is mobile, we can evaluate the effects when the adversary is either static or mobile. Under non-attack situations, the RSS trace from one node identity (i.e. one MAC address or one mote ID) is from one mobile transmitter. Under a spoofing attack, the RSS trace from one node identity is the mixture of two RSS traces from two different transmitters. We choose 20 m as the time window T of the RSS trace for both the 802.11 (Wi-Fi) network and the 802.15.4 (ZigBee) network. And the time interval is set to 1 s, thus there are total 1200 intervals (i.e. $n = 1200$) in our experiment.

5.3.1.2 Localization Algorithm

We used a scene-matching localization algorithm, called Gridded-RADAR [10], which builds an interpolated radio map to perform localization utilizing the reconstructed RSS traces in each time interval. There are two phases in the algorithm:

off line training phase and runtime testing phase. During the off line training phase, a mobile transmitter with known position broadcasts beacons periodically, and the RSS readings are measured at those four access points shown in Fig. 5.4. Collecting together the averaged RSS readings from each of the access point for 101 known locations, shown as small dots in Fig. 5.4, in our experiment provides an interpolated radio map, which serves as training data. During the runtime testing phase, localization is performed by comparing RSS values in the reconstructed RSS traces to the interpolated radio map. The record in the interpolated radio map whose signal strength vector is closest in the Euclidean sense to the observed RSS vector is declared as the location estimation.

5.3.1.3 Metrics

The effectiveness of the detection capability in DEMOTE lies in two aspects: accuracy and efficiency. We evaluate the detection accuracy in terms of the detection rate and the false positive rate. The detection rate is defined as the percentage of spoofing attack attempts that are determined to be under attack. We declare the presence of a spoofing attack when the computed value of the correlation coefficient is less than a threshold. Further, we define the detection time as the duration of a RSS trace that is needed to calculate the correlation coefficient for spoofing attack detection. The detection time versus the detection rate will be studied to evaluate the efficiency of DEMOTE.

5.3.2 Detection in Signal Space

5.3.2.1 Effectiveness

Figure 5.5 illustrates the reconstructed RSS traces for AP C under three different scenarios: a mobile wireless node under normal situations, under a spoofing attack with a static spoofing node, and under a spoofing attack with a mobile spoofing node. Figure 5.5a shows that under a normal situation the two reconstructed traces are changing together and reflect one movement pattern of the wireless node. We observed a high value of the correlation coefficient of 0.92. Under a spoofing attack, Fig. 5.5b and c show the RSS traces when the spoofing node is static or moving around respectively. In both figures we were able to extract two distinct RSS traces indicating two different movement patterns, and consequently the corresponding values of the correlation coefficient were low, only 0.1 and −0.19. Since the situation where a spoofing node is static is a very simple case to handle, we focus the rest of our discussion on the harder case where the spoofing node is mobile.

Figure 5.6 presents the values of the correlation coefficient of the reconstructed RSS traces from each AP for both the 802.11 network and the 802.15.4 network in normal situations and under a spoofing attack respectively. Under non-attack situations, we observed that the values of the correlation coefficient for both networks are consistently high across all access points, above 0.85. Whereas under a

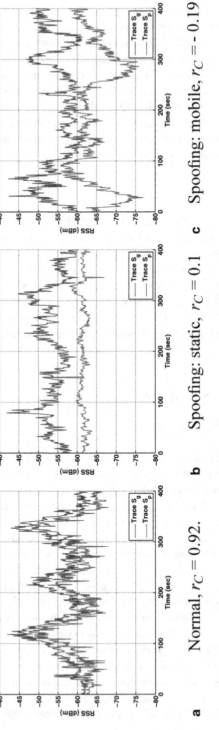

Fig. 5.5 The reconstructed RSS traces for access point C under different scenarios in the 802.11 network

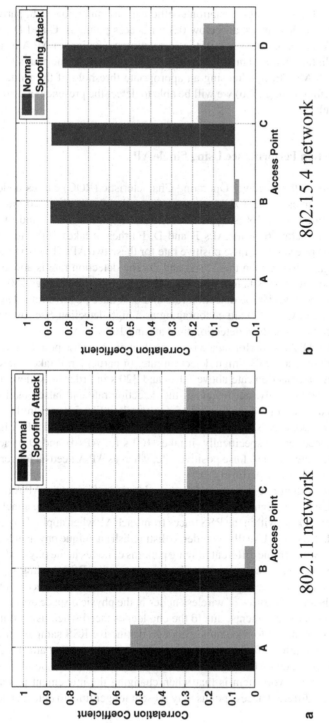

Fig. 5.6 The correlation coefficient of the reconstructed RSS traces for each access point

spoofing attack, the values of correlation coefficients are much lower. In particular, the correlation coefficients are all below 0.3 for access points B, C and D under a spoofing attack. However, the value of the correlation coefficient of AP A is around 0.5 which is slightly higher, but still much less than those under normal situations. Therefore, in DEMOTE, by choosing an appropriate threshold of the value of the correlation coefficient (e.g., 0.6) we will be able to detect the presence of a spoofing attack effectively.

5.3.2.2 Detection Performance Using Single AP

Figure 5.7 presents the Receiver Operating Characteristic (ROC) curves under different detection times in the 802.11 network for each AP. We observed that when the detection time is over 160 s, the detection rates are above 95 % and the false positive rates are below 6 % for APs B and D. Further, it takes 190 s to achieve 100 % detection rate and 0 % false positive rate for these two APs. The performance of AP C is slightly worse than the APs B and D. The detection rate is above 90 % and the false positive rate is below 6 % when the detection time is over 160 s. And it takes 200 s to achieve 100 % detection rate and 0 % false positive rate. Thus, the results from APs B, C, and D are encouraging as a high detection rate, over 90 %, can be achieved within a short detection time around 160 s.

However, for AP A, its performance is worse than other access points in terms of the detection time to achieve a high detection rate. In particular, it takes more than 270 s to achieve a detection rate above 90 % and 320 s in order to achieve 100 % detection rate. Additionally, our results of the detection rate and false positive rate versus various detection time for the 802.15.4 network in Fig. 5.8 are similar to that of the 802.11 network. APs B and D have the best performance and AP A has the worst performance. More specifically, it takes 160 s for APs B and D to achieve 100 % detection rate and 0 % false positive rate, whereas AP A needs a longer time, 320 s, to achieve the same performance.

This is inline with our observation of the correlation coefficient for AP A (around 0.5) in Fig. 5.6, which is higher than that from other APs under a spoofing attack. This indicates that bias exists within the RSS traces from each AP when applied to perform spoofing attack detection. Usually, in order to distinguish an unique physical location and consequently determine different moving patterns of nodes in the physical space, we need more than one access point to obtain a distinctive RSS reading in signal space. Using only one access point, we may observe similar RSS traces in signal space even if the moving traces of wireless nodes in the physical space are different.

Therefore, in our experiments, due to the challenges faced when using only one access point, AP A needs to accumulate enough distinctive RSS samples in signal space before it can infer different moving patterns under a spoofing attack. Consequently, we observed that AP A needs the longest time to detect the spoofing attack. An interesting future work item is that when changing the movement patterns of wireless devices, different access points may present longer time to detect an attack.

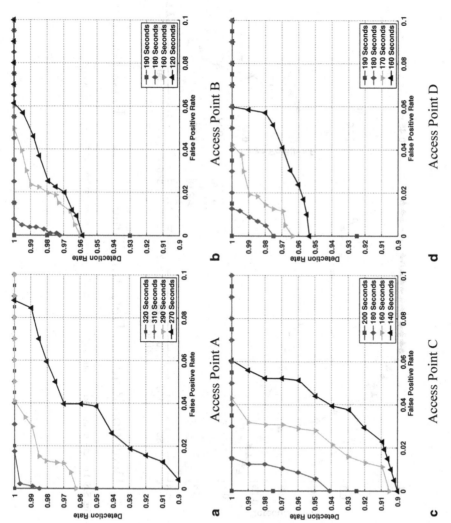

Fig. 5.7 ROC curves under different detection time for each AP in the 802.11 network

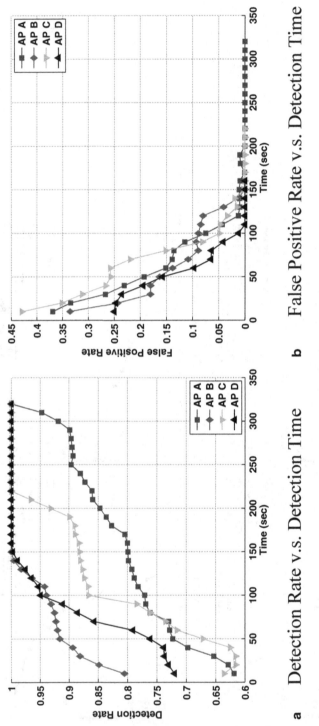

a   Detection Rate v.s. Detection Time

b   False Positive Rate v.s. Detection Time

Fig. 5.8 Detection rate and false positive rate as the function of detection time in the 802.15.4 network

5.3.2.3 Detection Performance Using Multiple APs

We further study how likely a spoofing attack can be efficiently detected by combing multiple APs. Suppose the value of the correlation coefficient of the reconstructed RSS traces from i^{th} access point is r_i, then the combined correlation coefficient of n access points is

$$r_m = \prod_{i=1}^{n} r_i. \tag{5.20}$$

We further normalize r_m as needed.

Figure 5.9a, b and c present the ROC curves under different detection time for the 802.11 network when combing 2, 3 and 4 access points, respectively. We observed that the detection rate increases and the detection time decreases when increasing the number of combined access points. Particularly, under the detection time of 80 s, the detection rate increases from 94 to 96.8 % and further to 97.7 % when the number of combined access points increases from 2 to 3 and to 4. Moreover, to achieve 100 % detection rate and the 0 % false positive rate, the detection time decreases from 160 s to 140 s and further down to 130 s when the number of combined access points increases from 2 to 3 and then to 4.

Figure 5.9d presents the comparison of the detection time when combining different number of access points for both the 802.11 network as well as the 802.15.4 network under the detection rate of 100 % and the false positive rate of 0 %. We observed that the detection time decreases sharply as the number of combined access points increases. Compared to using single AP for attack detection, the key observation is that the detection time is significantly reduced when using multiple APs. Particularly, we observed that the detection time reduced from 225 to 160 s in the 802.11 network and from 215 to 140 s in the 802.15.4 network. Further, the detection time decreases gradually when further increasing the number of multiple APs from 2 to 4. This is inline with our discussion in Sect. 5.3.2.2, that is, using a single access point cannot determine the unique location of a wireless device in the physical space, and thus using a single access point takes more time to distinguish the movement patterns for different nodes. Moreover, by using multiple APs the detection time presents a consistent decreasing trend indicating that the bias in RSS traces introduced by individual AP has been smoothed out. Therefore, combining multiple APs for spoofing attack detection helps to achieve a high detection rate and a low false positive rate quickly, which is a critical factor in a spoofing attack detection system such as DEMOTE.

5.3.3 Detection in Physical Space

In this section, we perform localization using the reconstructed RSS traces and study the spoofing attack detection capability of DEMOTE in the physical space.

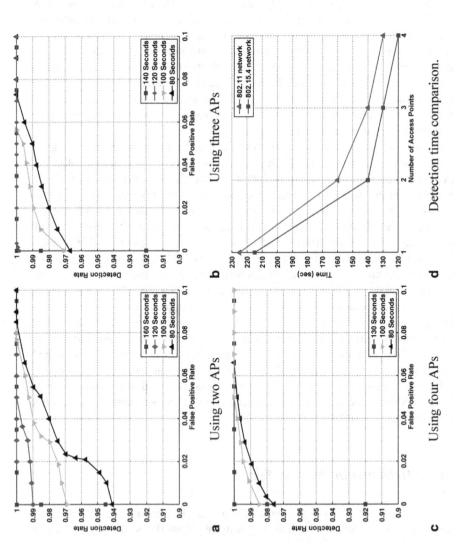

Fig. 5.9 (a), (b) and (c) are ROC curves under different detection time when using different number of access points for detection; (d) is the detection time versus different number of APs when achieving 100 % detection rate and 0 % false positive rate in both networks

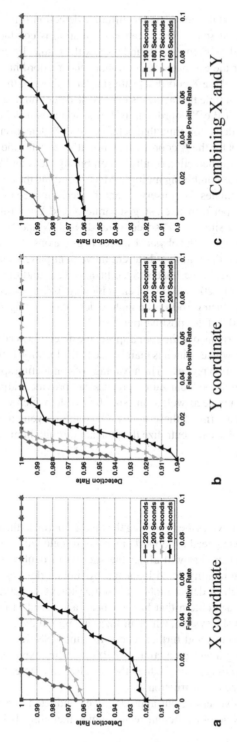

Fig. 5.10 ROC curves of detecting spoofing attacks in the physical space

Figure 5.10 presents the ROC curves under different detection time of detecting a spoofing attack in physical space. The location estimation is conducted using the Gridded-RADAR algorithm. Figure 5.10a and b show the results by calculating correlation coefficients over the estimated X coordinate and Y coordinate respectively. We found that the results of the X coordinate are similar to those of the Y coordinate. In particular, the detection time that achieves over 90 % detection rate with less than 6 % false positive rate for the X coordinate is 180 s, whereas it is 200 s for the Y coordinate. Further, the detection time that achieves 100 % detection rate and 0 % false positive rate is 220 s for the X coordinate, while it's 230 s for the Y coordinate.

Figure 5.10c presents the detection results by combining the X and Y coordinates. We use the same method as combining multiple APs to combine the correlation coefficients of X and Y coordinates. We observed that the performance of the combined results is better than the performance using separate X and Y coordinates. This is because our experimental site is a 2D space, it needs both X and Y coordinates to determine an unique location in the physical space. Thus we observed that the detection time is reduced when determining different movement patterns in the physical space by combining X and Y coordinates. Specifically, we found that the detection time can be reduced from 220 to 190 s when achieving 100 % detection rate and 0 % false positive rate and using 160 s is enough to detect a spoofing attack of about 96 % detection rate and 0 % false positive rate.

Compared to the performance in the signal space, the detection performance in the physical space is slightly worse, which is mainly due to the location estimation errors introduced by the localization process. The advantage of conducting spoofing attacks in the physical space is that the localization process can provide additional location information of the victim node as well as the spoofing node, which will further help to infer the movement patterns of these nodes. Once the movement pattern of the spoofing node is traced, one can neutralize the attacker through human intervention.

5.4 Summary

For many people mobile devices are becoming the favored portal to their online social lives. There is an increasing need to support emerging mobile wireless applications. One serious class of threats that will affect the successful deployment of mobile wireless applications are identity fraud launched by mobile devices. In this work, we proposed an approach to detect mobile spoofing attacks in pervasive wireless environments, which is a problem that has not been addressed in previous work. We developed the DEMOTE system, which utilizes an optimal thresholding scheme to partition the RSS readings and further reconstruct the RSS traces over time for attack detection. Our alignment prediction (ALP) algorithm exploits the temporal constraint in the RSS readings and predicts the best RSS alignment of partitioned RSS classes for RSS trace reconstruction.

To validate the effectiveness of our approach, we conducted experiments using mobile wireless devices across different technologies including IEEE 802.11 b/g and IEEE 802.15.4 in an office building environment. We investigated the detection performance of DEMOTE in terms of detection accuracy and detection efficiency both in the signal space, using either single access points or multiple access points, and in the physical space, using the localization results. Our experimental results provide strong evidence that our system and algorithm is highly effective and efficient in detecting spoofing attacks in mobile environments. Further, we found that under normal (non-attack) situations the reconstructed RSS traces are highly correlated since the traces are originated from one mobile device, whereas under a spoofing attack the RSS traces are much less correlated because of the presence of the spoofing node that is not moving together with the victim node.

References

1. F. Ferreri, M. Bernaschi, and L. Valcamonici, "Access points vulnerabilities to dos attacks in 802.11 networks," in *Proceedings of the IEEE Wireless Communications and Networking Conference*, 2004.
2. J. Bellardo and S. Savage, "802.11 denial-of-service attacks: Real vulnerabilities and practical solutions," in *Proceedings of the USENIX Security Symposium*, 2003, pp. 15–28.
3. D. Faria and D. Cheriton, "Detecting identity-based attacks in wireless networks using signalprints," in *Proceedings of the ACM Workshop on Wireless Security (WiSe)*, September 2006.
4. Q. Li and W. Trappe, "Relationship-based detection of spoofing-related anomalous traffic in ad hoc networks," in *Proceedings of the Third Annual IEEE Communications Society Conference on Sensor, Mesh and Ad Hoc Communications and Networks (SECON)*, September 2006.
5. Y. Chen, W. Trappe, and R. P. Martin, "Detecting and localizing wirelss spoofing attacks," in *Proceedings of the Fourth Annual IEEE Communications Society Conference on Sensor, Mesh and Ad Hoc Communications and Networks (SECON)*, May 2007. (Acceptance rate: 20
6. Y. Sheng, K. Tan, G. Chen, D. Kotz, and A. Campbell, "Detecting 802.11 MAC layer spoofing using received signal strength," in *Proceedings of the IEEE International Conference on Computer Communications (INFOCOM)*, April 2008.
7. T. Sohn, A. Varshavsky, A. LaMarca, M. Y. Chen, T. Choudhury, I. Smith, S. Consolvo, J. Hightower, W. G. Griswold, and E. de Lara, "Mobility detection using everyday gsm traces," in *UbiComp*, September 2006, pp. 212–224.
8. K. Muthukrishnan, M. Lijding, N. Meratnia, and P. Havinga, "Sensing motion using spectral and spatial analysis of wlan rssi," in *EuroSSC*, October 2007.
9. J. Krumm and E. Horvitz, "Locadio: inferring motion and location from wi-fi signal strengths," in *MOBIQUITOUS*, Aug 2004, pp. 4–13.
10. K. Kleisouris, Y. Chen, J. Yang, and R. P. Martin, "The impact of using multiple antennas on wireless localization," in *Proceedings of the Fifth Annual IEEE Communications Society Conference on Sensor, Mesh and Ad Hoc Communications and Networks (SECON)*, June 2008.
11. R. Redner and H. Walker, "Mixture Densities, Maximum Likelihood and the EM Algorithm," *SIAM Review*, vol. 26, p. 195, 1984.
12. R. C. Gonzalez and R. E. Woods, Digital Image Processing. Prentice Hall, 2007.
13. N. Otsu, "A threshold selection method from gray-level histograms," *IEEE Transactions on Systems, Man, and Cybernetics*, vol. 9, no. 1, pp. 62–66, 1979.
14. K. Fukunaga, *Introduction to Statistical Pattern Recognition*. Academic Press, 1990.
15. M. Mancas, B. Gosselin, and B. Macq, "Segmentation using a region-growing thresholding," in *Proc. SPIE*, vol. 5672, 2005, pp. 388–398.
16. F. Scheid, *Schaum's Outline of Theory and Problems of Numerical Analysis*. McGraw-Hill, 1989.

17. Y. Chen, J.-A. Francisco, W. Trappe, and R. P. Martin, "A practical approach to landmark deployment for indoor localization," in *Proceedings of the Third Annual IEEE Communications Society Conference on Sensor, Mesh and Ad Hoc Communications and Networks (IEEE SECON)*, September 2006.
18. I. Miller and J. Freund, "Probability and statistics for engineers," *PRENTICE-HALL, INC., ENGLEWOOD CLIFFS, NJ 07632(USA), 1984, 530*, 1984.
19. G. Casella, R. Berger, and R. Berger, *Statistical inference*. Duxbury Press Belmont, Calif, 1990.

Chapter 6
Related Work

The traditional approach to prevent spoofing attacks is to use cryptographic-based authentication [1–3]. [1] has introduced a secure and efficient key management framework (SEKM). SEKM builds a Public Key Infrastructure (PKI) by applying a secret sharing scheme and an underlying multicast server group. [2] implemented a key management mechanism with periodic key refresh and host revocation. to prevent the compromise of authentication keys. An authentication framework for hierarchical, ad hoc sensor networks is proposed in [3]. However, the cryptographic authentication may not be always applicable because of the limited resources on wireless devices, and lacking of a fixed key management infrastructure in the wireless network. In addition, binding approaches are employed by Cryptographically Generated Addresses (CGA) to defend against the network identity spoofing [4].

As it is not always desirable to use authentication due to limited resources on nodes and infrastructural overhead involved, recently recently new approaches utilizing physical properties associated with wireless transmission to combat attacks in wireless networks have been proposed. Based on the fact that wireless channel response de-correlates quite rapidly in space, a channel-based authentication scheme was proposed to discriminate between transmitters at different locations, and thus to detect spoofing attacks in wireless networks [5]. [6] focused on building fingerprints of 802.11b WLAN NICs by extracting radiometric signatures, such as frequency magnitude, phase errors, and I/Q origin offset, to defend against identity attacks. However, there is additional overhead associated with wireless channel response and radiometric signature extraction in wireless networks. [7] introduced a security layer that used forge-resistant relationships based on the packet traffic, including MAC sequence number and traffic pattern, to detect spoofing attacks. The MAC sequence number has also been used in [8] to perform spoofing detection. Both the sequence number and the traffic pattern can be manipulated by an adversary as long as the adversary learns the traffic pattern under normal conditions.

The works [9–11] using RSS to defend against spoofing attacks are most closely related to us. [9] proposed the use of matching rules of signalprints for spoofing detection. [10] modeled the RSS readings using a Gaussian mixture model. [11] proposed to use the node's "spatial signature", including Received Signal Strength

J. Yang et al., *Pervasive Wireless Environments: Detecting and Localizing User Spoofing*,   67
SpringerBriefs in Computer Science, DOI 10.1007/978-3-319-07356-9_6,

Indicator (RSSI) and Link Quality Indicator (LQI) to authenticate messages in wireless networks. However, none of these approaches are capable of determining the number of attackers when there are multiple adversaries collaborating to use the same identity to launch malicious attacks. Further, they do not have the ability to localize the positions of the adversaries after attack detection.

Turning to studying localization techniques, in spite of its several meter-level accuracy, using RSS [12–15] is an attractive approach because it can reuse the existing wireless infrastructure and is highly correlated with physical locations. Dealing with ranging methodology, range-based algorithms involve distance estimation to landmarks using the measurement of various physical properties such as RSS [12, 13], Time Of Arrival (TOA) [16], Time Difference Of Arrival (TDOA) and direction of arrival (DoA) [17]. Whereas range-free algorithms [18] use coarser metrics to place bounds on candidate positions. Another method of classification describes the strategy used to map a node to a location. Lateration approaches [16], use distances to landmarks, while angulation uses the angles from landmarks. Scene matching strategies [12] use a function that maps observed radio properties to locations on a pre-constructed signal map or database. Further, [19] proposed to perform detection of attacks on wireless localization and [17] proposed to use the direction of arrival (DoA) and received signal strength of the signals to localize adversary's sensor nodes. In this work, we choose a group of algorithms employing RSS to perform the task of localizing multiple attackers and evaluate their performance in terms of localization accuracy.

The work discussed in this book differs from the previous study in that we use the spatial information to assist in attack detection instead of relying on cryptographic-based approaches. The proposed approach is novel because none of the exiting work can determine the number of attackers when there are multiple adversaries masquerading as the same identity. Moreover, our proposed method can detect spoofing attacks in mobile wireless environments. Additionally, our approach can accurately localize multiple adversaries even when the attackers varying their transmission power levels to trick the system of their true locations.

References

1. B. Wu, J. Wu, E. Fernandez, and S. Magliveras, "Secure and efficient key management in mobile ad hoc networks," in *Proceedings of the 19th IEEE International Parallel and Distributed Processing Symposium (IPDPS)*, 2005.
2. A. Wool, "Lightweight key management for ieee 802.11 wireless lans with key refresh and host revocation," *ACM/Springer Wireless Networks*, vol. 11, no. 6, pp. 677–686, 2005.
3. M. bohge and W. Trappe, "An authentication framework for hierarchical ad hoc sensor networks," in *Proceedings of the ACM Workshop on Wireless Security (WiSe)*, 2003, pp. 79–87.
4. T. Aura, "Cryptographically generated addresses (cga)," *RFC 3972, IETF*, 2005.
5. L. Xiao, L. J. Greenstein, N. B. Mandayam, and W. Trappe, "Fingerprints in the ether: using the physical layer for wireless authentication," in *Proceedings of the IEEE International Conference on Communications (ICC)*, June 2007, pp. 4646–4651.

6. V. Brik, S. Banerjee, M. Gruteser, and S. Oh, "Wireless device identification with radiometric signatures," in *Proceedings of the 14th ACM international conference on Mobile computing and networking*, 2008, pp. 116–127.
7. Q. Li and W. Trappe, "Relationship-based detection of spoofing-related anomalous traffic in ad hoc networks," in *Proceedings of the Third Annual IEEE Communications Society Conference on Sensor, Mesh and Ad Hoc Communications and Networks (SECON)*, September 2006.
8. F. Guo and T.-c. Chiueh, "Sequence number-based mac address spoof detection," in *Recent Advances in Intrusion Detection*, 2006, pp. 309–329.
9. D. Faria and D. Cheriton, "Detecting identity-based attacks in wireless networks using signalprints," in *Proceedings of the ACM Workshop on Wireless Security (WiSe)*, September 2006.
10. Y. Sheng, K. Tan, G. Chen, D. Kotz, and A. Campbell, "Detecting 802.11 MAC layer spoofing using received signal strength," in *Proceedings of the IEEE International Conference on Computer Communications (INFOCOM)*, April 2008.
11. L. Sang and A. Arora, "Spatial signatures for lightweight security in wireless sensor networks," in *The 27th IEEE Conference on Computer Communications (INFOCOM)*, 2008.
12. P. Bahl and V. N. Padmanabhan, "RADAR: An in-building RF-based user location and tracking system," in *Proceedings of the IEEE International Conference on Computer Communications (INFOCOM)*, March 2000, pp. 775–784.
13. E. Elnahrawy, X. Li, and R. P. Martin, "The limits of localization using signal strength: A comparative study," in *Proceedings of the First IEEE International Conference on Sensor and Ad hoc Communcations and Networks (SECON 2004)*, Oct. 2004, pp. 406–414.
14. Y. Chen, J.-A. Francisco, W. Trappe, and R. P. Martin, "A practical approach to landmark deployment for indoor localization," in *Proceedings of the Third Annual IEEE Communications Society Conference on Sensor, Mesh and Ad Hoc Communications and Networks (IEEE SECON)*, September 2006.
15. J. Yang and Y. Chen, "A theoretical analysis of wireless localization using RF-based fingerprint matching," in *Proceedings of the Fourth International Workshop on System Management Techniques, Processes, and Services (SMTPS)*, April 2008.
16. P. Enge and P. Misra, *Global Positioning System: Signals, Measurements and Performance*. Ganga-Jamuna Pr, 2001.
17. Z. Yang, E. Ekici, and D. Xuan, "A localization-based anti-sensor network system," in *26th IEEE Conference on Computer Communications (INFOCOM)*, 2007, pp. 2396–2400.
18. T. He, C. Huang, B. Blum, J. A. Stankovic, and T. Abdelzaher, "Range-free localization schemes in large scale sensor networks," in *Proceedings of the Ninth Annual ACM International Conference on Mobile Computing and Networking (MobiCom'03)*, 2003.
19. Y. Chen, W. Trappe, and R. P. Martin, "Attack detection in wireless localization," in *Proceedings of the IEEE International Conference on Computer Communications (IEEE INFOCOM)*, April 2007.

Chapter 7
Conclusions and Future Work

The advancement of wireless technologies allows us to share information gathered by wireless devices and makes it available to users to consume or process on-the-go. However, the security of the underlying wireless networks is a major hurdle that needs to be overcome in order to achieve the successful and widespread deployment of pervasive wireless networks supported by the vast array of emerging wireless technologies. This book is focused on enhancing wireless security by exploiting spatial correlation information to enhance wireless security in pervasive wireless environments.

We first started with examining the user spoofing attack since it is especially harmful as the claimed identity of a mobile device is often considered as an important first step in an adversary's attempt to launch a variety of attacks. We proposed an attack-detection model that utilizes the spatial correlation of Received Signal Strength (RSS) inherited from wireless devices. We then developed statistical approaches to determine the number of attackers when there are multiple adversaries masquerading as the same identity. Moreover, we integrated our attack detector into a real-time indoor localization system, which can also localize the positions of the attackers even when attackers using different transmission power levels. We conducted experiments on two testbeds through both an 802.11 network (Wi-Fi) and an 802.15.4 (ZigBee) network in two real office building environments. We found that our detection mechanisms are highly effective in both detecting the presence of attacks with detection rates over 98 % and determining the number of adversaries, achieving over 90 % hit rates and precision simultaneously. The performance of localizing adversaries achieves similar results as those under normal conditions, thereby, providing strong evidence of the effectiveness of our approach in detecting wireless identity-based attacks, determining the number of attackers and localizing adversaries.

Furthermore, we developed the DEMOTE system to detect identity fraud attacks in mobile wireless environments. The developed DEMOTE system exploits the correlation within the RSS trace based on each node's identity to perform attack detection in either the signal space or the physical space. Our approach does not require any changes or cooperation from wireless devices other than packet transmissions. Through experiments from an office building environment, we show that

J. Yang et al., *Pervasive Wireless Environments: Detecting and Localizing User Spoofing*, 71
SpringerBriefs in Computer Science, DOI 10.1007/978-3-319-07356-9_7,
© The Author(s) 2014

DEMOTE achieves accurate attack detection both in signal space as well as in physical space using localization and is generic across different technologies including IEEE 802.11 b/g and IEEE 802.15.4.

Our research work serves as a pioneer's effort to explore using the unique wireless property, spatial correlation, as a useful characteristic associated with each wireless device to address security problems. The proposed research work highlights the importance of new paradigms for securing future wireless systems that takes advantage of unique wireless-specific properties to thwart security threats without requiring overhead to wireless devices.

We envision there is a broad array of characteristics that are unique to wireless communications, which have not been exploited but might be used to enhance the security of wireless systems, such as the location of communicating devices, the characteristics of radio propagation. Based on this vision and current results in this book, we think it is important to address future directions in the following.

Using spatial correlation of RSS inherited from wireless devices can enhance the security of pervasive wireless networks. However, the RSS-based method subjects to the limitation of distance between two wireless devices. RSS-based detection method is not working well when two wireless devices are very close to each other. To mitigate this limitation, one further research direction is to combine the unique properties of RSS correlation with traditional cryptographic means to secure the wireless networks. For example, in wireless mobile environments, such as mobile ad hoc networks, it is hard to maintain a central authority to distribute and manage the keys. However, by exploiting the properties of wireless channel between any two parties is unique and decorrelates rapidly in space, two users can establish a common cryptographic key from RSS readings without replying on a central authority to distribute or manage the keys. In addition, by exploiting the RSS readings from multiple channels, we expect to push the limitation of distance between two wireless devices as short as possible. Moreover, besides the spacial correlation of RSS, some other unique properties of wireless communication, such as channel frequency response and channel state information in OFDM, are also in consideration for enchanting security of pervasive wireless networks when such channel information are made available in commercial off-the-shelf wireless devices.